The Heart in 1
an exploration of the roots of human love and social cohesion

Dr Amali Lokugamage

Images:

Cover: Laraine Krantz, Ritapix, London. "Not in the head, but in the heart"

Page 42: © Réunion des musées nationaux, France/Gérard Blot.

Page 42: Ajit Mookerjee Collection. From Kali: The Feminine Force, Ajit Mookerjee, Thames & Hudson Ltd., London.

Page 85: Laraine Krantz, Ritapix, London. "Reflexology with Gowri"

Page 115: Laraine Krantz, Ritapix, London. "Sharing Love and Knowing"

Edited by Lindsay Porter

Cover design: Crispin Chetwynd & Fran O'Connell

Page design: Crispin Chetwynd & Fran O'Connell

First Printing: 2011

Published by Docamali Ltd.

ISBN: 978-0-9569667-0-4

CONTENTS

The Heart in the Womb

Amali Lokugamage was born in Sri Lanka but brought up in the United Kingdom. Her early education was in London. She has a BSc (Medical Science) from St Andrews University, an MBChB from Manchester University, an MD from University College London and an MSc in Epidemiology from the London School of Hygiene and Tropical Diseases. She is a Fellow of the Royal College of Obstetricians and Gynaecologists (FRCOG) and a consultant obstetrician and gynaecologist at a hospital in London. She has authored several peer-reviewed scientific papers on research studies in women's health.

Amali has done tsunami relief medical work in Sri Lanka and India. She is also a trained homeopath and acupuncturist, with a keen interest in meditation. She helped to set up a maternity acupuncture service in her hospital and also has an integrated medical gynaecology practice for chronic gynaecological conditions. Amali is married and has a son born as a homebirth.

ACKNOWLEDGMENTS

With thanks to my husband, and my parents, who helped care for my baby whilst I wrote this book. My son was my inspiration. He gave me fresh insights about childbirth and led me to an inner wisdom about birthing. I am also grateful to hugging amma for helping me to embrace motherhood.

FOREWORD

By Dr Luke Zander

When teaching medical students, I frequently asked how they would define the difference between obstetrics and pregnancy, and was fascinated to observe the difficulties they initially had in answering that question. Their uncertainty is a striking example of the fundamental questions surrounding our understanding of the birth process and the importance of how we undertake the delivery of maternity care. To what extent do the objectives and aspirations of obstetric care relate to those of pregnancy and childbirth? Much of the controversy arising in the field of maternity care is a result of the potential conflicts inherent in these differing perspectives.

There is no denying the enormous advances that have taken place in our scientific understanding of many aspects of the birth process, and in the changes that have been introduced regarding the provision of maternity care. These have resulted in very significant improvements in many highly sought-after parameters of care. The major focus of this care has been to seek ways to reduce risk and to improve outcome by the development of means to prevent, identify, monitor and manage any real or potential complications of the birth process. As a result, a highly risk-averse approach to healthcare has developed.

This approach, with all its obvious or apparent benefits, is generally seen as completely rational when viewed through the eyes of the providers of obstetric care, and there is an inevitability about the direction in which this approach is likely to proceed if left unchallenged and unchecked. However, it is important to recognise that it contains within it significant dangers, including a limited awareness about what is relevant or significant from the perspective of the pregnant woman.

Today, there is a greater awareness of a holistic and woman-centred approach to healthcare, and most professional care-givers will state that this is what they aim to provide. However, such claims may often be based on a misunderstanding and lack of appreciation of the scope of what these terms can mean. The practice of "whole person" medicine involves more than taking account of an individual's wishes and belief systems concerning the way they might want their birth to be managed, but is instead an appreciation of the bio-psycho-social dimensions of medicine, and the inter-relationships that exist between them.

Such an approach is all too frequently missing in our present-day, rather mechanistic, protocol-determined approach to the delivery of healthcare, where the essential focus of our efforts is to reduce risk of morbidity and mortality rather than to enhance quality of experience and health.

Numerous studies have provided compelling evidence for the influence of different factors – physical, psychological and emotional – on the process of birth, and on the importance of the birth process to the mother, her child and wider society. Many of these studies, however, remain outside the domain of the obstetric literature. This book explores many of these fundamental issues, and provides thought-provoking ideas and highly relevant insights into the process and experiential dimension of the birth process.

An important and significant aspect of the book is that it is written by an obstetrician who has modified and enhanced her insights and understanding of the process of childbirth and its management as a result of her own experience. Although remaining rooted in the field of practical obstetrics, the author moves away from the confines of its way of thinking to embrace new approaches and concepts drawn in part, from the realm of complementary medicine – in which she is a trained expert – and from Eastern culture.

Describing the emotional and attitudinal changes that she experienced in her journey through pregnancy and childbirth, Amali Lokugamage draws together ideas and evidence from many disciplines and perspectives, all of which are highly relevant to our understanding of the birth process and its effects.

This book provides much food for thought for all those concerned with the planning and provision of maternity care, as well as for women wishing to learn about the wide range of sources of help and support during pregnancy and childbirth. Amali Lokugamage has written a fascinating, informative and thought-provoking book that will kindle a wider perspective of the birth process and its experiential dimension.

Luke Zander was the founder of the multidisciplinary Forum on Maternity and the Newborn at the Royal Society of Medicine, and a founder member of the Association of Community-based Maternity Care. He was an advisor to the Parliamentary Select Committee on Health, under the chairmanship of Nicholas Winterton, for its report on maternity services. He is a past advisor to the National Perinatal and Epidemiology Unit in Oxford and to the National Childbirth Trust, and is a past President of the General Practice Section at the Royal Society of Medicine.

PART 1
AN EXPERIENCE OF BIRTH

CHAPTER 1
INTRODUCTION

To have the opportunity to give birth in a comfortable, supportive, natural way is a life-enhancing event. Birth can be an empowering experience, and although a natural process may not always be possible due to specific circumstances, even to attempt it brings great richness to a woman's life. The power of the feminine, in turn, enriches society and has a much wider impact than on just the individual.

Modern-day life and our highly stressed, "risk-averse" society have led to a medicalised, fearful model of childbirth, which has stripped the process of its wondrous magic. As an obstetrician, I have always been tremendously proud of the role of western medicine in improving the safety of childbirth. But in recent years I have become aware that somehow medicine, in the process of reducing hazards and attempting to decrease the possibility of litigation, has disempowered women, and with that has come a parallel loss of balance in pregnancy care. I see this in my professional capacities as obstetrician and gynaecologist, epidemiologist, medical researcher, acupuncturist and homeopath, and through my knowledge of various strands of ancient Eastern medicine. I have come to understand that, by reducing the hazards for a small number of people or for rare, severe illnesses, we actually risk interfering with the normal health of greater numbers of people, potentially converting their situation to abnormality, and thereby creating illness. This is a difficult tightrope to walk. Perhaps, as with the recommendations of the World

Health Organisation[1] for a caesarean section rate threshold of 10–15%, which balances saving lives with causing iatrogenic (medical) harm, we should consider an appropriate threshold in risk-reduction strategies that reduces mother and baby illness or death, but also takes into account illness created by over-medicalised births. An implicit assumption in risk-reduction health policy is to catch or prevent illness before it results in a poor outcome for the mother and baby. Such an assumption has intuitive appeal. Yet the concept of health prevention interventions, e.g. screening for diseases, is not as straightforward as it may first appear, as such practices can cause harm as well as being of benefit.[2] Certainly, interventions or practices that lead to the psychobiological ill health of the individual, which eventually combine and have a knock-on effect on societal health, can be particularly hard to keep track of. Pregnancy and birth are areas of health where mind-body interactions are very important to the proper physiological function of the body via hormones such as natural oxytocin.

My own pregnancy transformed my views of childbirth. Until then, my knowledge had been derived from academic tomes on obstetrics, epidemiological studies, statistics of childbirth, and the "traditional" beliefs of obstetricians derived from twenty years of obstetric practice in the United Kingdom. But these views were radically revised following my own experiences. However, this knowledge can only truly have been accessed during pregnancy because it is based on the non-material, immeasurable inner wisdom that pregnancy hormones unlock in a woman's consciousness. These changes slow down left-brain-orientated rational thoughts and open a portal into greater right-brain activity, which offers women amazing gifts of consciousness that are normally suppressed in everyday modern life. The forgetful pregnant brain is an asset to birthing well, as it naturally dissipates the anxieties that accompany strategising and "over-thinking", because it is geared towards allowing awareness to rest in the present moment. Contemporary women often rebel against this state of mind, as it is particularly difficult to succumb to it whilst working and it is not well supported by modern society. However, in the field of mindfulness psychotherapy there is growing support for the idea that this state of mind reduces stress and related physical diseases. There are cognitive therapies aimed at facilitating this consciousness through practise and conscious effort; however, nature itself endows this state to pregnant women – if only they are able to surrender to it.

Before and during my pregnancy, I was lucky enough to hear and meet some of the most experienced and knowledgeable non-medical birthing gurus. These are internationally renowned natural childbirth experts or birth activists whom I later mention in chapter 6. My colleagues in clinical medicine and medical research have, for the most part, been completely unaware of the existence of these other experienced birthing experts, but, for me, their input into my pregnancy was invaluable. My standard medical antenatal care was supportive, but the experience of these alternative pregnancy-care gurus was empowering, as their knowledge-base helped me to access my own inner wisdom and inner confidence to birth well.

The words "consciousness" and "inner wisdom" may mean nothing to my fellow obstetric colleagues because they are more preoccupied with material ways of preventing illness and death in mothers. But birthing well is undeniably linked to mind and body health, as shown by studies demonstrating that the presence of an older "wise" woman providing support to the mother during childbirth has a greater effect on helping the woman to achieve a normal, safe birth than many standard medical interventions. This suggests that improving a woman's emotional status and confidence in her body to undergo childbirth is as important as having a medical infrastructure. The French for midwife, "sage femme", literally means "wise woman", a term that acknowledges the role of this supportive figure. Fear of childbirth and lack of confidence in the body's ability to face the process are factors that have been linked to the increase in requests for caesarean sections. Similarly, lack of privacy and birthing environments that produce fear have been linked to inefficient womb contractions, leading to the need for medical deliveries. These are not the only factors contributing to such outcomes, but they are currently deeply underestimated in contemporary hospital-based maternity systems.

This book is a commentary of my observations and experiences, both

Right Brain-Left Brain. This illustration symbolises the differences in thought processes when decision-making.

as an obstetrician and a pregnant woman. For an obstetrician to have a homebirth is a rarity, and it is because of this that I feel I can provide a unique commentary on my own experience, from both a professional and a personal viewpoint. I stress, however, that this is not a scientific book; it is more about the art of birthing and I have approached the book through my experience of living. I was prompted to write about this very personal experience because, prior to my pregnancy, I was never fully able to understand why a woman would actively choose to give birth at home, outside of a hospital safety-net. However, during my own pregnancy I became increasingly aware of the fact that once a woman taps into her innate birthing wisdom, decision-making no longer takes place only through logical risk-analysis, but instead though an internal – call it perhaps an instinctual – knowledge of what is right for herself and her baby. If this voice from within is very strong – and during pregnancy it can become very strong indeed – then it overrides any logical argument. The expectant mother develops a courage and confidence towards childbirth and an awareness that, if she is in a comfortable setting, her body will know how to let the natural process unfold.

Robbie Davis-Floyd, childbirth medical anthropologist, says "women giving birth undergo a quite powerful and psychologically compelling physiological and cognitive transformation."[3] This is because pregnancy is a time of great change for a woman's body and mind, which creates opportunity for personal growth. In my case it caused an internal revolution whereby I questioned my previously unshakeable beliefs, and which I now regard as a rite of passage. Traditionally, rites of passage entail a period of liminality in which the initiate is considered dangerous to society because he or she is living in a transitional realm between social categories that is not officially acknowledged. This threatens the entire underpinning of the culture, yet, if properly handled, can be culturally revitalising, as is borne out by my own experience.[4] Despite being an expert in the field of medical birth, this liminal state compelled me to decide against a medical setting for giving birth. Although writing this book may unsettle the obstetric status quo, it may also kindle a wider perspective of meaningful birth.

My pregnancy re-crafted my understanding of birthing and its profound effect on the emotional programming of society at large. Child and, consequently, adult behaviour is moulded by the environment of pregnancy and birth. Quite literally, our ability to love, trust, be generous and socially competent is sculpted by the birth process, which inspired the title *The Heart in the Womb*. Medicine tends to treat birth as a technical episodic event that has to be made safe. However, in parallel streams of science, sociology and psychology, there have been new discoveries about the longstanding societal impact of birth, which somehow have not managed to penetrate mainstream medical or midwifery knowledge. In a sense, we doctors have tunnel vision regarding motherhood. This book urges us to look to the horizon and beyond.

The Heart in the Womb unfurls in three parts. The first part relates to my own homebirth experience. The second discusses the theatrical stage for the players who influence birth practices: the doctors, midwives and doulas. The third part reflects on the gains that normal birth can provide for the mother in respect of her attitude to child rearing and to her life as a mother, thereby enhancing the emotional lives of her children. It is also about the potential wider impact of natural birth on the emotional fabric of society and how natural birth may set society's behavioural tone. This section of the narrative offers some of the growing evidence that natural mechanisms of normal birth are enormously important in the biological, behavioural programming that deepens our ability to give and receive love.

This book celebrates the unappreciated skill of Mother Nature through normal birth to create social cohesion and to remedy a fragmented and destructive society. This is especially relevant to future planetary survival, as issues such as climate change, overcrowding and limitation of natural resources will test our ability to live together harmoniously.

CHAPTER 2
AN OBSTETRICIAN'S HOMEBIRTH STORY

CONCEPTION TALES

My path to pregnancy was an unusual one for an obstetrician and gynaecologist. I married rather late in life and then, in the early days of my marriage, used my holiday leave from my job as a consultant obstetrician to become very involved in tsunami relief work. However, after leaving the last medical camp in the Tamil Nadu, India, I fell ill, probably because of the sheer volume of patients that I had seen in fairly extreme climatic conditions. In the field, my colleagues and I worked in 40-degree heat and saw at least 120 patients during each half-day clinic, in very remote, rural settings. We hadn't factored in any rest time after the relief work and returned to a full work schedule back in England. As a doctor, I had become accustomed to pushing myself to work beyond the limits of exhaustion – a sort of culture amongst medics. Yet after this illness, I developed a non-specific fatigue syndrome and wasn't quite my usual energetic self. As these symptoms lingered, I found that it was taking me a long time to conceive. I was over forty years old and therefore my chances of conceiving were low. Following medical fertility tests, I was astonished and saddened to discover I was nearing menopause. My sense of grief is shared by other women in this situation, and wasn't helped by the fact that, in such cases, standard medical gynaecological treatments, such as in vitro fertilisation and other assisted conception techniques, generally have very poor success rates.

However, because I am an acupuncturist and I am familiar with the principles of traditional Chinese medicine (TCM) and its theories governing fertility, I knew that I had other options. Chinese herbs and acupuncture can help in some areas of fertility problems, such as:

- Helping ovulation in women who are peri-menopausal.
- Increasing fertility in women with polycystic ovarian syndrome.
- Improving the quality of both eggs and sperm.
- Improving the lining of the womb, and endometriosis.
- Helping to regulate hormones.

Although the theory and practice of acupuncture and TCM have been tried and tested over thousands of years, there is now some observational scientific data that backs up these theories.[5-10] More research is needed in this area, but research grants for complementary medicine are difficult to come by in Britain. This is a huge topic, however, warranting a book in itself, so is beyond the scope of this title.

I followed a course of acupuncture and traditional Chinese herbs, along with continuing my usual practice of daily meditation supplemented with self-hypnotherapy CDs, which helped me to relax and provided some useful visualisations. Very soon afterwards, I started to ovulate again, as was evident from my basal body temperature charts and blood tests. The herbs, which contain lots of antioxidants, are reputed to improve the quality of the egg released at ovulation, helping to repair cell damage and reduce the risk of Down's Syndrome which increases with the age of the mother. Although there is no scientific evidence proving beneficial qualities of Chinese herbs in human females, there is a genetic study showing that the chromosomal quality of sperm improves with Chinese fertility herbs.[11] Three months into this treatment, I became pregnant. It was not all plain-sailing, however: as with any type of natural medicine where the modus operandi consists of helping the body to harmonise itself, I had to tolerate several detoxification symptoms to get my system fertile again. This is quite different from current allopathic practice, where symptoms are contained or discomforts suppressed by drugs. In complementary medicine, detoxification symptoms or healing aggravations are a type of curative pathway. I had physical symptoms related to improving the energy in my kidneys, and emotional symptoms related to improving the blood supply to my uterus and ovaries. According to TCM, the energy of the kidney and its meridians is very important for fertility, as the kidney governs libido and ovarian/testicular function. There is no parallel concept in Western medicine, except that as human beings form as embryos, the kidney and the ovaries or testes originate from the same type of tissue. In TCM, sensory organs may be related to internal organs, such as the ear to the kidney. At this time leading up to conception, after a very strong acupuncture treatment, I developed acute right middle-ear infection (otitis media). I wanted to avoid using antibiotics and paracetamol as I knew from experience that the ear infection was part of a healing pathway to fertility, and although the drugs would have alleviated my symptoms, they may have impeded the kidney energy detoxification reaction. Instead, I treated the infection with herbs and homeopathy, and once it had settled and cleared, I found myself pregnant in my next cycle.

THE DESTRUCTION OF OLD IDEAS

As soon as I conceived my son, I lost autonomy over my body. The baby just took over all my systems. Intellectually, I knew this would happen, but it was quite difficult to contend with the full extent of it in practice. It was only in retrospect that I realised this was the perfect experience to transform me from being a very driven, creative, and highly academic woman, to one that was completely soft, unworried and pliable in mind and body, allowing for a beautiful homebirth. In my former state, and because of the mental programming that had become ingrained in me over the last twenty years of professional medical experience, I would only have considered a hospital delivery. Obstetric practice and the experience of seeing some terrible pregnancy disasters have led quite a few of my colleagues to request elective caesarean sections instead of embarking on a vaginal delivery, let alone a homebirth. And yet, this letting go of the rational mind, and embracing an innate, physical mindfulness during pregnancy, set me on the path to a homebirth.

In my professional life I have observed that certain personality types find it very difficult to have a totally natural delivery. Generally, over the age of twenty-five, such women are used to being in control of all aspects of their lives ("control freaks") and therefore can find labour, a time when nature takes over and being in complete control is impossible, a source of great anxiety. Being able to take events as they come, with the mind focused on the present moment, is a positive emotional attribute that helps labour to proceed in a more graceful manner. Under the age of twenty-five, a woman's body is flexible and often works well to birth naturally, without any particular preparation. Later, the body and mind slowly start to rigidify and certain physical and mental habits are formed. This can influence pregnancy outcome, especially if it is a woman's first baby. From a medical perspective, there are several research studies demonstrating that aging in women is associated with various pregnancy problems, some of which relate to developing illnesses that occur through advancing age, such as heart disease.[12] Age can also affect the mechanism of childbirth, causing, for example, inefficient uterine action (uterine dystocia) and rigidity of the pelvic tissues. Complementary medicine interprets the process of aging and its effect on pregnancy through the idea that tissue can hold the cellular memories of unresolved life experiences and ancestral disease blueprints, although there is nothing in western science to support this. Both TCM and the ancient Indian practice of Ayurvedic medicine are based on the principle that the aetiology of illness arises from both the emotions and predispositions of the individual, as well as their environment. There is ample psycho-neuro-immunological or psycho-biological medical data to demonstrate how profoundly the mind affects physical health.[13] There is a series of case histories gathered by psychologists and the popular press supporting this theory, including the fascinating personal account of Claire Sylvia, the recipient of a heart transplant, who has published her experiences claiming she inherited the dietary habits and emotions of her donor.[14] This is not an area that can be easily tested by quantitative research, so we may never be able to reach a definitive scientific verification of this cellular memory phenomenon, but recent research, published in the high ranking science journal *Nature*, suggests that single cell organism may demonstrate cellular memory.[15]

From the moment I became pregnant, circumstances made it very difficult for me to work. I was overjoyed to be pregnant and felt that I had many tools to help me enjoy it, but the pregnancy had its own agenda, one that ultimately meant I had to stop attempting to steer my pregnancy in the direction that I initially thought was best. I soon realised, through inner communication with my baby, that he had his own ideas of what was in his best interests, and he was a great teacher.

From the beginning of the menstrual cycle that I conceived in, I developed a slightly painful left shoulder and following that, severe nausea and vomiting – hyperemesis – from eight weeks' gestation. I have used acupuncture successfully to treat many women with nausea and vomiting in pregnancy, which is supported by scientific evidence,[16] but in this instance I found that I was unable to cure myself. I used the maternity acupuncture service at the hospital and also asked my husband, one of the best acupuncturists I know, to treat me, but my nausea just got worse. Like many pregnant women, I was keen to avoid using drugs, and as I have a fairly high discomfort threshold, I just put up with the symptoms, managing to keep up my fluid levels and taking myself to bed as the symptoms became more severe, encouraged throughout by the love and support of my husband.

After a few weeks in bed, and probably due to my lack of mobility, my left shoulder became frozen, which made it impossible to carry out the manual part of my job. I have used acupuncture to treat many of my patients with frozen shoulder and found excellent improvement in symptoms, but once again I was unable to cure myself. Physiotherapy treatment only made the shoulder worse, with the pain becoming excruciating after sessions of even gentle mobilisation. The pain of my frozen shoulder was worse than any labour pain that I subsequently experienced. At this time, there were no curative medical treatments for this condition and all the data seemed to indicate that frozen shoulders simply follow their own natural course, taking months to cure. I felt quite bewildered by my symptoms.

The nausea and vomiting eventually started to settle after about 17 weeks' gestation, during which time I found comfort in conferring with pregnant friends who had suffered similar symptoms. I had hoped that the hyperemesis would stop at the 12th week and was disheartened when this was not the case, but my friends who had experienced it before had all had to wait until 17–20 weeks before their symptoms improved. I had wanted to do yoga during this time, but had experienced severe motion sickness with any sort of movement and was limited until the frozen shoulder became less painful. In all, I felt worn out and exhausted. I also felt quite guilty that I was not able to work, but the situation seemed quite out of my control: the frozen shoulder made work and examining patients impossible. At the same time, my own obstetrician was waiting for a glucose tolerance test because of a family history of diabetes, but I had been unable to keep down the sugar for the test. This was further delayed by an outer ear infection that came and went of its own accord, and which I'm sure was a little echo of what I had had before, probably exacerbated by my fragile immune system and low nutritional levels due to vomiting. Infections affect the accuracy of glucose tolerance tests, so the procedure had to be postponed for a couple of weeks until the ear infection had cleared. By now I had enormous sympathy for my patients who were ill during pregnancy, particularly the hyperemesis women.

During this time I began to notice that I became slightly forgetful, as if my brain had gone a bit foggy, or "soft". Many pregnant women speak of this phenomenon and researchers have found that pregnancy hormones such as oxytocin can affect certain learning and memory functions.[17;18] Before I was pregnant, I could hold quite a lot of statistical mathematics in my head and could calculate sample-size equations very snappily, but after about 10 weeks' gestation I noticed a great void in my statistical ability. Colleagues asked me to evaluate a scientific paper in my area of research but I really struggled to bring forth the concentration and the logical thought process required for the critique. And it was not only my brain that had gone soft: except for my left shoulder, my body had too. I was surprised that I had become very sensitive to firm beds and hard chairs. It was a bit like the tale of the *Princess and the Pea*, in which a princess is so sensitive that she can easily detect a pea placed at the bottom of one hundred blankets. I hadn't ever been taught about this in my medical training, but later in pregnancy yoga sessions my teachers confirmed it was a very common experience for pregnant women. My solution was to get a memory-foam mattress-topper and lots of cushions to support my body whilst lying in bed, a place where I spent increasing amounts of time. This "softening" of mind and body, and the inability to rush around and be active really beat the "yang" masculine part of my personality out of me. My husband saw me change from a self-sufficient woman to a much softer version of myself. He seemed to enjoy it despite the fact his workload had increased looking after me.

At this point in time I had also noticed that, although I had nausea and vomiting, my abdomen was becoming more and more bloated. I looked far more pregnant than I was, and the abdominal distension was restricting my diaphragm and making it more and more difficult to breathe. I had also started to experience discomfort in my right leg, probably because I could only lie on my right side in bed. So, when one night I woke up and it felt as though all the air in the room had emptied – a feeling of "air hunger" – I took myself to hospital to check that I hadn't developed a pulmonary embolus, or blood clot on the lungs, which is an obstetrician's fear for pregnant women and one of the main causes of maternal deaths in England.[19] It was during this brief hospital admission that I noticed two crucial things: one was that labour wards were agitated places and not at all restful; the second was that there seemed to be a very tangible feeling of an inner communication between the baby and me.

Whilst I was being assessed on the labour ward, an environment with which I am very familiar in my working life, I became increasingly aware of how little the ward is conducive to peace and tranquillity. The doors of the ward are frequently kept ajar because the midwives look after several women at once, and it is easier for them to hear when they are needed. However, this also means the women are aware of all the surrounding business on the ward, such as the cries of distress of labouring women or the drama of someone being rushed to the operating theatre for a caesarean section. There was often a tap on the door and people coming and going on other hospital business: re-stocking cupboards, borrowing equipment for another room, etc. It made me feel "edgy" as a patient, and I realised that if a woman was in labour in hospital, aiming for a comfortable, safe environment to enable her body to work with nature, the agitated atmosphere in the labour ward would expose her to the antithesis of this, which would trigger the release of her "fight or flight" body chemicals, adrenaline and noradrenalin. These chemicals would slow down womb contractions, disturbing the natural rhythms set up by her own body.[20] I realised that if it felt that way for me as a doctor, in a familiar setting, surrounded by known and trusted colleagues, it must be far worse for patients.

Whilst I was being assessed and was waiting to undergo medical tests, I also became aware of what I can only describe as emanations of energy coming from my baby telling me he was not happy for me to be in the hospital. I really felt his personality; it was a very subjective feeling, but nonetheless, very real. Many pregnant women describe communicating with their baby and although there is scientific proof that babies respond to the sound of their mothers' voices,[21;22] there is very little scientific evidence of communication going the other way, although this makes emotional sense.

However, there are plausible physiological explanations for this, from neurological, immunological and endocrine perspectives. There are also pregnancy-linked immune-mediated and endocrine (glandular) illnesses that are precipitated by fetal/placental factors such as pre-eclampsia or gestational diabetes. The HeartMath Institute in the United States has done some research on mother and baby heart communication.[23;24] In fetal development, the rudimentary heart is one of the first organs to start developing: the hearts in both fetus and adult produce a subtle electromagnetic field which, in the case of mother and child, envelop each other. The heart is not only a pump, but also has numerous neurological connections both within the heart and outside of it, via neural networks to the brain's limbic area, and the rest of the body via the spinal cord and the peripheral nervous system.[25] The heart also has an endocrine function, regulated by hormones.[26] Animal studies have revealed oxytocin receptors in embryonal heart cells, and oxytocin is a hormonal mediator of love.[27;28] We know that electromagnetic fields can influence each other: fetus upon the mother and the mother upon the fetus. We also know that there can be increases in cardiac and psychiatric-related hospital admissions due to changes in the earth's electromagnetic field, secondary to solar events such as sunspots.[29,30] Furthermore, the electromagnetic field of incubators in neonatal intensive-care units can influence heart rate variability in newborns.[31] So mother and baby are interlacing magnetic fields and could exert effects on one another.

Anyhow, getting back to my pregnancy, luckily all my medical tests were normal and one of my obstetric medicine colleagues said that, through a process of elimination of other medical causes, it was likely that my breathlessness had been caused by my respiratory centre re-setting because of pregnancy. She was familiar with the condition and sees it in a few women every year. The symptoms soon abated, helped by a yoga-breathing technique, but I was left with the feeling that somehow my baby had expanded the capacity of my heart and that the breathlessness and chest discomfort were symptoms of my emotional heart being stretched beyond its comfort zone.

It was at this time that I spoke to my friend Françoise Barbira Freedman, founder of the Birthlight yoga movement, who told me about a wonderful book, *Mother's Breath*, by Uma Dinsmore Tuli.[32] I read it avidly and followed its yoga-breathing exercises. Yoga-breathing for pregnant women is very different from standard yoga-breathing techniques, and the advice in the book really helped my breathing and ability to relax. In conjunction with this, my shoulder became less painful, which allowed me to contemplate doing pregnancy yoga.

At this time I also got to know Dr Gowri Motha and her Gentle Birth Method, and I feel I reached a turning point in my pregnancy when, following the Gentle Birth Method, practising yoga with Françoise Barbira Freedman and attending the Active Birth Centre founded by Janet Balaskas, I actually got better.[33] (This is discussed in more detail in Chapter 6.) For the first time I understood the value of being gentle to my body. The experience really opened my eyes to aspects of pregnancy care that were totally absent in the standard medical approach, however holistic I had thought it was.

At 19 weeks gestation I finally had my glucose tolerance test done, which revealed I had gestational diabetes. I wasn't surprised, as both my parents have type 2 diabetes, a condition to which Asians, especially after middle age, are particularly susceptible. But I was also coming to realise that all my pregnancy ailments thus far were echoes of the health problems that my mother had had when she was just a few years older than me. It was as if my pregnancy was bringing my ancestral illnesses to the fore. With this diagnosis, my occupational health doctors recommended that I should not return to work for the remainder of my pregnancy. I found this very difficult to accept because I had always expected to continue to work to some degree throughout my pregnancy. It is amazing how one can be so attached to work despite one's health problems. However, I know now that if I had had the opportunity to return to work and renew my obstetrics blueprints, I probably would not have undergone the consciousness changes that I had in the later part of my pregnancy and that led to my homebirth.

In complementary medicine, there is a concept that the first layer of health to be addressed is one's personal emotional and physical biography. The next layer addresses ancestral blueprints of disease, which are brought to the fore in order for the body to activate its self-healing mechanisms. Each layer of complementary medicine seeks to prompt the body to shed its aberrant cellular mechanisms, recall how to make the cells work properly, and essentially activate self-healing. It is not uncommon for symptoms to worsen temporarily before they get better in order to detoxify the body. Therefore, the emergence of all my ancestral diseases did not surprise me. Standard medicine offered no quick fixes for them, and in the end I managed to overcome their patterns without having to suppress and contain them. My gestational diabetes, for instance, got better rather than worse over time, which contradicts the conventional view that gestational diabetes intensifies as the placenta grows larger.

I gradually realised that the first part of my pregnancy, with all its adverse symptoms, was really about the destruction of old patterns; my baby was determined to birth in his own way and for that I needed to learn a bit more about pregnancy. I thought of myself as a fairly well-rounded doctor who used standard medicine for life-threatening problems but who could also counsel patients with chronic or slowly evolving illnesses about standard medicine options, as well as a few complementary ones. I had lectured publicly about how birth preparation is very important in helping mothers to overcome their fears and to improve their pelvic soft tissues to make the birth easier. But somehow, up until this point in my own pregnancy, the idea of mothers being gentle with themselves – of society allowing them to be so during pregnancy – and, indeed, the whole concept of nurturing the expectant mother, had been, for me, more of an intellectual concept than a felt truth. The second half of my pregnancy was about renewal and the emergence of inner wisdom and communication with my baby, which was really facilitated by the huge amount of nurturing I received. In Sri Lanka where I was born, there is a very strong tradition of women nurturing pregnant women and mothers. My pregnancy really helped me connect to the benefits of this tradition.

CROSSING A BRIDGE TO ANOTHER BIRTHING WORLD

The next part of my pregnancy saw the re-emergence of a new kind of power, a softer strength. I threw myself into the Gentle Birth Method and accepted the nurturing it provided me. Gowri had so much wisdom to offer, and the pregnancy yoga (Birthlight and Active Birth) helped me to accept the changes that had occurred, and regain confidence in my body to birth.

I have had many types of massage in my life, but the first "creative healing" massage I had from Gowri used a technique that was incredibly nurturing, and so was well suited to pregnancy. Up until now I had felt very toughened by a life in medicine; this massage really opened my eyes to a method of facilitating gentleness and relaxation in a mother. My early pregnancy symptoms had left me feeling so ravaged that I had lost the knack of relaxation. Gowri did a long session of creative healing massage and reflexology. She diagnosed my episode of extreme shortness of breath as heart related, which she treated with a specific "heart" creative healing massage. She also advised me to stop eating wheat, and to take a calcium/magnesium supplement and digestive enzymes to reduce the bloated abdomen. I was initially doubtful about the wheat intolerance theory but was soon converted when, after following her advice, the bloating subsided.

The use of evidence-based medicine can be beneficial in sieving through which treatments are helpful and which are not, but it is limited and is not the only helpful way of determining how best to promote healing in people. Some non-clinical doctors as well as scientists, economists and politicians can become caught up in the number-crunching game of statistics and lose sight of what actually heals people or promotes well-being. Complex treatments where no placebo can be introduced can never truly be assessed by the gold standard research methodology of randomised controlled trials. Often, in the competitive field of research grant application, it is difficult to raise funds to undertake research in non-fashionable areas of health. In order to be a good doctor rather than a research scientist, experience is paramount, especially in areas where physical and emotional needs overlap: the "human touch" counts for a lot in healing the patient. Gowri's audit statistics for the Gentle Birth Method[34] seem to indicate that it serves women well. From the first visit I made to her practice rooms, I overheard women with babies enthusing about their amazing births, a side to childbirth that obstetricians don't hear much about. An obstetric postnatal visit typically addresses and answers questions about problems that arose during the birth, so it was very refreshing to hear wonderful, life-affirming stories. The women also talked about how the whole programme made them feel healthy, fit and emotionally prepared to give birth. The more I heard, the more enthusiastic I became about trying the system for myself. I really wanted to have the kind of birth these women were describing and wanted to do everything I could to help myself achieve it. I knew from experience that a natural birth is not guaranteed by following any particular system, but to get oneself "birth fit" tips the balance in favour of a positive journey towards birth and a more positive outcome.

Conventional maternity care systems currently offer antenatal health monitoring, quick chats with health professionals about welfare, antenatal classes about the mechanism of labour and what medical interventions are available if needed. Our system provides reassurance or crisis management if required but doesn't really offer nurturing or emotional preparation for birth. Nor does it offer advice about preparing the body's tissue for birth. Even though it is the aspiration of the NHS to offer flexible, individualised services, resource limitations mean that care is usually delivered according to certain protocols, except in unusual cases. The Gentle Birth Method has a different approach to the process of birthing and offers body preparation systems that incorporate nutritional advice, herbs, food supplements, oils, exercise and yoga, and emotional preparation strategies, such as nurturing the mother, education, confidence building, self hypnosis and visualisations. In addition, the Gentle Birth Method offered treatment to help me overcome gestational diabetes, whereas the standard medical approach is to restrict carbohydrates or, if that doesn't work, to administer tablets or insulin injections. I had sessions of acupuncture from my husband and had the "pancreatic" creative healing massage to get my blood sugar under control. There is an animal study[35] and numerous articles in Chinese medical journals showing the beneficial effect of acupuncture on patients with type 2 diabetes, but as of yet, there have been no studies from non-Chinese research centres on using acupuncture for this purpose, nor research on "pancreatic" massage techniques.

Towards the end of my pregnancy my blood sugars returned to normal, which allowed me to contemplate a homebirth. Usually in pregnancy, gestational diabetes worsens as the placenta grows, which is why so many women with diabetes in pregnancy have an induction of labour to safeguard against any ill effects of poor sugar control.

As the pregnancy advanced, hormones carried on the softening process in my body and my ligaments became overly elastic, causing me to develop pubic symphysis and sacro-iliac displacement as my joints clunked in and out of position, making it increasingly difficult to walk. Once again, pregnancy yoga was a saving grace, allowing me to stay mobile as well as I could and giving me confidence to birth. It was now clear, with every new symptom, that my baby wanted to keep me from rushing around at my usual hectic pace, and my condition was pushing me ever closer to that inner space of birthing wisdom and peace. I went to local pregnancy yoga classes at the Active Birth Centre (ABC)[36] in London, and found it very useful to network with other mums in my area and to discover what services and resources were available nearby. Lyn Murphy's classes at the ABC helped me to stretch gently, to breathe, to be present with my baby, and to accept the softening of my mind and body. But I also went to classes led by my inspirational friend Françoise Barbira Freedman in central London, whose insight helped me to be much more active than I could have hoped for, given the pain in the pubic symphysis area. Her dynamic style of pregnancy-adapted yoga, breathing, meditations and incorporation of yoga dance, along with her instinctive ability to read the personalities and responses of babies to their mothers' yoga, brought out a courageous joy of pregnancy in me.

Pelvic girdle dysfunction is the current official term for a constellation of symptoms that result from excessive softening of the pelvic ligaments. Symphysis pubic dysfunction and pubic separation are all former names of conditions that fall under this banner term. It can be treated with physiotherapy, in which case the strategy is to give advice about the causes of the condition, suggest exercises and physical manoeuvres to limit the dislocation of the pelvic bones, and limit the physical tension placed on areas that are uncomfortable. A physiotherapist can arrange for the provision of support apparatus such as hip and abdominal girdles, walking sticks, or even a wheel chair if necessary. Pregnancy yoga can still be done, but when there is pubic pain, certain movements are not recommended by the majority of yoga teachers. However, during my classes, I found that, although it is certainly sensible to limit certain movements, those muscle groups that become inactive start to collect tissue toxins through lack of use, and the stagnation of these substances in the muscles leads to significant pain, too. It occurred to me that, somehow, these muscle groups should not be allowed to remain completely inactive. This is where I found great help in the Birthlight approach to individualised assessment of a woman's yoga needs, and its use of yoga dance using diagonal rather than parallel moves.

During my childhood I learnt Sri Lankan dance and drumming. It is a very dynamic and strong art form that became hardwired into my system, and whose techniques and moves my body has retained. In my early adult years I extended my interest in dance and drumming to Latin American styles such as Salsa, Cuban-style percussion and Brazilian Samba. Françoise's use of yoga dance unlocked the almost primordial motor patterning in me, where I found that, although walking was very painful, I could somehow, quite elegantly, complete a number of the yoga dance moves. She further discovered that I could do the basic Samba dance moves quite swiftly and beautifully, despite being unable to walk properly, which was quite bizarre for any onlookers to observe. Françoise recounted to me that, "In spite of the extreme SPD, you were able to dance wonderfully in the yoga classes, amazing all the other women with the grace of your swift steps... no one could quite believe you were the same woman, one moment with a face contorted with excruciating pain, the next moment smiling in this ancient dance!"

In his book *Awakenings*, neurologist Dr Oliver Sacks describes paradoxical neurological phenomena such as catatonic depressive patients who are completely immobile until stimulated by a very individualised action, which enabled them to leap up suddenly and catch a ball, before dropping back swiftly into their stiffened, unresponsive state. Dr Sacks describes such examples as "paradoxical tales, for neurological disease can conduct one to other modes of being that – however abnormal they may be to our way of thinking – may develop virtues and beauties of their own."[37] The virtue and beauty that I discovered through Birthlight yoga was that, although I could not walk, I could rely on my own inner neurological, emotional, energetic and physical hard-wiring of Asian dance to get me through labour. Perhaps that aspect of me was chiselled into my right-brain activity (which was certainly beginning to dominate at this stage in my life), whereas walking was more allied to my left-brain activity. This gave me a lot of inner peace and the confidence to allow my body to unfold its innate programming to give birth using my own good qualities.

So gradually, over the course of my pregnancy, my attitude towards birthing changed. Before pregnancy, although intellectually I was an advocate of natural birth, I did not fully compute why women would want to go to a birthing centre or have a homebirth. I believed that natural birth could happen in a hospital, supported by the benefits of modern medicine if necessary. Why would anyone want to give birth in a location without this safety net? I interviewed women who had elected for homebirth and a common response was a fear of hospitals and a lack of confidence that their bodies would work well in that environment. Many thought that the hospital environment was stressful; they feared hospital-acquired infections or they had had a traumatic hospital experience in the past. Others said they knew instinctively that their bodies could give birth and they wanted to be in a comfortable environment to get on with it, or they had birthing confidence because of an easy first birth. Many perceived that homebirth midwives were more experienced than the average midwife, and they liked the idea of the midwife coming to them rather than them having to travel to a hospital midwife. They also perceived that if there were a problem in labour, the transfer to the hospital would be fairly smooth and swift. Above all, these women described the greater sense of personal empowerment experienced through a normal birth at home.

At the time, I couldn't really resonate with these attitudes at an intellectual level. It was almost like describing colours to a blind person, and in this respect I was typical of the average British consultant. In the current NHS system, midwives are present at the trouble-free births, whereas we consultants have our perception skewed, our horizons blotted out, by our experiences with complicated pregnancies or deliveries. However much meditation I had done in the past or intuitive ability I had developed with experience of all types of medicine, it was only during the second half of my pregnancy, when the pregnancy hormones influenced my brain, that I really developed an affinity with the idea of birthing centres and homebirth. Other pregnant doctors may not have drawn these conclusions, but they would probably not have had the chance to immerse themselves in the experiences that I had, such as pregnancy yoga, Birthlight principles, the Gentle Birth Method and Active Birth ideology or, as I will discuss in Chapter 6, to listen to great speakers such as the renowned midwife and author Ina May Gaskin or commentators on the impact of birth, child and human development such as Michel Odent, Frederick LeBoyer and Joseph Chilton Pearce. Before my pregnancy, I was unfamiliar with Michel Odent's theory about the "scientification of love".[38] I had not encountered the basic human and animal studies that indicated that the pulsatile manner of oxytocin release in a mother during pregnancy may have an influence on her capacity to love and nurture. These ideas are not widely discussed in the field of obstetrics, despite there being enough basic data to warrant investment into detailed research, with its potentially enormous impact on the behaviour of society. Much of my research was on the use of drugs to promote uterine contractions for labour and also to prevent bleeding after childbirth.[39-44] I had been immersed in the salient literature regarding the science of helping the uterus to contract, but had never encountered Odent's ideas in these publications or at any obstetric conference. Pulsatile oxytocin is "the love hormone". If it promotes altruism and is at its highest levels just before vaginal birth, then helping women to reach that natural state has a potentially very far-reaching impact on promoting these emotional qualities within society.

At a professional and a personal level, the more antenatal visits I had, the more I noticed the unavoidable consequence of risk-reductive medicine, which leads to an atmosphere of nervous tension and fear in the system: fear of causing harm, fear of the consequence of ignorance, fear of missing a clinical sign and fear of litigation. I was also aware of the use of technology at the expense of hands-on medicine to streamline clinic visits, such as using ultrasound scan reports exclusively, rather than in conjunction with abdominal examination. Medical consultations are increasingly spent scrutinising laboratory reports, graphs or tables of biochemistry, with less time for the human aspect of the consultation. This is an entirely necessary part of the delivery of medical care, but with the advent of more and more technology and the sheer volume of patients that need to be seen, this human side to the consultation is being increasingly marginalised. Doctors do "care" for their patients, but technology, protocols and guidelines have eaten into the time that should be dedicated to individualised human rapport, leaving midwives to deal with the more humanistic side of care delivery. I came to really love my midwife antenatal checks, which helped me to address some very basic "new mum" queries, such as how to deal with pregnancy forgetfulness, how to get more comfortable in bed with the aid of cushions/pillows/pads or where to begin looking for the right sort of pram. One particular

National Institute of Clinical Excellence (NICE) guideline that I felt was absurd and that contributes to the de-humanisation of antenatal consultations, is the recommendation not to listen to the fetal heart because of a lack of evidence of any benefit.[45] With more time spent on risk-reduction strategies and less on human interaction, the simple check of the baby's heartbeat redresses this imbalance, restoring the wonderful human aspect of appropriate touch from the caregiver, and providing reassurance to the mother and time for bonding with the baby. Listening for the fetal heart was one of the loveliest parts of the antenatal check.

During this time, my inner communication with my baby continued to grow and I felt as though he was unhappy whenever I went into the hospital. Gradually he seemed to pulse the idea of a homebirth into my thinking space. I also sensed him telling me that he knew how to birth himself and that all I needed to do was surrender to the process and be in as relaxed an environment as possible. I became aware that the personality of the baby does not start from the moment he or she is born, but is evident before birth, in the womb. Why should it suddenly appear after birth? I now believe that some babies – although not all – with strong personalities can enter the consciousness of their mothers and steer the perinatal environment. The psychobiology of the intra-uterine environment is an area of new expanding research and there is much to explore.

I was initially hesitant to bring up the subject of homebirth because the usual medical advice, given my age and risk factors, would be to recommend against it. It was also very dependent on the state of my health in the last trimester of pregnancy. But I felt comfortable bringing up the possibility with my midwife, Rachel Ambler, a consultant midwife at my hospital who had been involved with my pregnancy from the outset and was easy to talk to, offering me continuous emotional support throughout my pregnancy. Rachel had a lot of experience with homebirths and my hospital had an excellent homebirth midwifery team. She suggested that I have a chat with them and see how they operated. The other midwife that I had asked to take part in my care, Kim Singh, was also very experienced at homebirths. I had observed Kim on the labour ward in my capacity as a consultant, and her silent, supportive care, presided over many normal births. I often saw that she stayed in the labour room continuously, but did not chat unnecessarily to the labouring woman. She was often silent, arranging and re-arranging her equipment trolley, seeming simply to wait for the labour to unfold , whilst quietly and unobtrusively carrying out the usual intrapartum checks.

Some natural-birth gurus say that this silent, supportive, instinctive style helps the woman to utilise her inner knowledge to deliver the baby. Constant interruption, even chatting, causes anxiety during labour, which in turn causes a woman's body to lose the natural rhythm it sets up to produce pulsatile oxytocin for efficient contractions, as well as preventing the relaxation needed to allow maximum stretchiness of the soft tissue of the pelvis. The birthing environment should be dimly lit and comfortable, and the woman must be confident that she has the necessary support without it disempowering her. Having been a labour ward obstetrician for many years, I hadn't until now, fully appreciated how a ward-round entourage entering a labour room could be so disturbing to the mother. Many of the women that I met during my pregnancy who had had their babies described this feeling when they met doctors on the labour ward. They also described the phenomena of their contractions dwindling when a subjectively perceived, unsupportive doctor or midwife entered their room. Peripartum emotional support is very important in helping the mother to achieve the best of her body's capability.

I was invited to join the homebirth-team's coffee mornings, which I hadn't known about before, and where I met many very empowered women who had taken responsibility for their health, knew the potential of their own bodies and their babies, and who had wanted to labour at home. The women that had previously given birth at home or in an un-medicalised fashion recounted such lovely stories of their births. Some women achieve quite transcendent states of mind in labour and their stories were very uplifting to hear. But integral to the discussion about how they had decided on a homebirth was the question of risk, with the overwhelming conclusion being that many activities in ordinary life can be risky, and yet to avoid them for fear of the risks involved would prevent us from fully engaging in the richness of life itself. We used the analogy of crossing a busy main road in an urban environment, which can be very dangerous. We could choose not to cross the road to guarantee we would feel safe, but this would mean never really participating in our environment and essentially becoming a prisoner of our own safety issues. Giving birth is a normal part of life; it only involves disease – and therefore requires medical intervention – in the minority of cases. To miss out on a potentially transformational life experience through fear of crossing the road was not in the mindset of these women.

As an obstetrician exploring the art of birthing, I was both fascinated and inspired. I would never have otherwise encountered this forum as part of my extended working environment. Homebirth midwives said that, in their experience, any problems that might appear in homebirth labours tend to evolve slowly over time, and are picked up on well before they reach critical levels because the mother is attended by one midwife throughout labour, rather than by shifts of different midwives, as with the hospital system. During a homebirth, there are usually two midwives present at the birth itself. The whole process is very low tech, using anywhere at home as the birthing area. It is up to the woman how she waterproofs the area and structures the environment to best suit her needs and wishes. Homebirth midwives are very flexible.

Following these conversations I wanted to find more about water births, which is an area obstetricians have very little expertise or knowledge of. Typically, obstetricians feel that water birth is non-traditional, even unnatural. Their experience is limited to assessing water births where there has been a problem, but they are not able to comment on the many water births that have gone well. At the time of my pregnancy, there was very little research in this area except for observational data from Switzerland.[46] However, the information from this research study does show that women who have had water births had less pelvic trauma and less blood loss, and that there was no difference in infection rates between water and land births.

To find out as much as possible from an expert in the field, I attended one of Janet Balaskas's water-birth workshops at the Active Birth Centre in London. This excellent workshop provided me with new knowledge that water is a great non-medical pain-relief option for labour, but that it can slow down as well as speed up a labour. According to Janet Balaskas's experience, if immersion in water is done too early in labour (less than 5cm dilation) then the relaxation that can ensue may slow contractions and prolong the labour. However, if used after 5cm dilation it frequently, in her experience, shortens the labour. Janet Balaskas advises that, if possible, a woman seeking a water-birth should aspire to remain active, upright and mobile, using other non-medical forms of pain relief until she reaches 5cm or more. As a woman seeking a non-medicalised birth, I was motivated to explore as many modes of non-medicalised relaxation and pain relief as were available. I have always liked investigating any type of healing treatments. I do not resist unfamiliar ideas or non-traditional methods simply because they do not follow the principles that I have been taught, are outside of the current scientific paradigm or because they have not been sufficiently researched. I believe one should always be on the look-out for anything that makes the patient feel better, and not sabotage it with any medical prejudice. After all, Copernicus had a very hard time convincing people that the Earth orbited around the Sun, as it went against the prevailing paradigm that the Earth was at the centre of the universe.

At this time, I remembered two of my male doctor colleagues advising me against natural birth. One of them was particularly worried about the prospect of a homebirth for me. The other said that he would recommend an elective caesarean section. I reflected how technical and risk-based their rationale was and how far removed they were from considering birth to be an amazing experience. To explain my perspective would, to use the analogy again, have been like describing colours to a blind person. But I, too, have been in their camp and fully understood where they were coming from.

PREPARATION FOR HOMEBIRTH

The more yoga, breath meditation and nurturing by the Gentle Birth Method I experienced, the more I felt an inner rapport with my baby. I felt he was much stronger than me and knew what he wanted for his well-being; he definitely wanted a homebirth. My inner wisdom concurred with this and I knew that if I had a hospital birth I would be at high risk of being on a conveyor belt of medical interventions because of my age and risk factors, not to mention the fact my colleagues would be overly cautious in looking after me because I was an obstetrician. I had a hunch that my baby would launch himself out before the increased medical surveillance from 38 weeks' gestation, in sheer effort to avoid a hospital birth. This prediction proved to be correct and my labour started a few days after 37 weeks. My blood sugars gradually corrected themselves with acupuncture and pancreatic massage and towards the end of my pregnancy they were perfectly normal. My mental and physical softening deepened. I often forgot to lock my car, neglected to switch off the stove and was unable to retain any theoretical information. At the same time, my pelvic ligaments were soft, which made it very painful to walk, and yet I was in a strange state of unworried bliss. I found that the less analytic thought, worry and strategising I experienced, the more my instinctive maternal wisdom about the birth process came to the fore. After all, normal birth is programmed into a woman's nature.

Rachel Ambler and Kim Singh agreed to attend my birth. The fact they were very senior midwives went some way to allay the fears of my obstetricians. Even though I myself am an obstetrician, I booked myself into some independent midwifery antenatal classes run by some other midwifery colleagues. The classes, called "Birthing Matters"[47] were excellent and a good way of educating my husband about the physiological process of birth and usual hospital care in case we had to go there. It was also good to be at the receiving end of antenatal classes and to experience being a pregnant woman hearing the midwifery philosophy.

I went to a very informative Birthlight yoga workshop for couples, where my husband and I were coached about helpful birthing postures, breathing, relaxation, massage techniques and yoga sounds to utter to open up specific areas of the pelvis. Sounds such as "Aa" open up the front of the pelvis and pubic area and sounds like "Oh" can help open up the back of the pelvis. Depending on the way the baby is facing and the birthing position of the mother, these sounds can be quite useful. The principle is as follows: in yoga the jaw and mouth have a harmonic relationship with the pelvis. If the jaw is clenched then the pelvis is tense, and if the jaw is opened then the pelvis relaxes and opens out. Ina May Gaskin calls this the "sphincter law", where she has found that a relaxed mouth and jaw directly correlate with the ability of the cervix and vagina to open fully. Following this principle it is possible to breathe the baby out, rather than actively pushing. This knowledge is not part of routine medical or midwifery practice, where the valsalva manoeuvre of closing the mouth, pursing the lips and straining down on the pelvis is often advised by traditionalists. I had never even heard of the notion of breathing the baby out until I had done pregnancy yoga, but it is also one of the techniques used in pregnancy hypnosis for birthing. There are parallels with the idea of relaxing versus straining due to constipation. If the bowels are normal then straining is not required as relaxation and an upright position allows the sphincters to open and the bowels to move. Breathing a baby out is not dissimilar. It is dependent on good womb contractions. Standard antenatal classes do not teach this particular technique.

To minimise vaginal and perineal trauma during delivery and to reduce postnatal pain, I learnt a daily vaginal massage technique from Gowri Motha. Again, standard antenatal education has little to say about this practice, but there is good scientific evidence supporting its benefits.[48] Most practitioners advise starting the massage in the third trimester and Gowri was very specific about the technique she found most beneficial. Rather than massaging the vaginal lips/perineum from side to side as advocated by some, she said it was much better to gradually stretch the vagina toward the pelvis bony wall at four, six and seven o'clock (where the clitoris is regarded as 12 o'clock) - deepening the stretch each day, until there is no stinging sensation. The full technique is described in her book.[34] She always advises that the area is first treated with a special Ayurvedic vaginal oil that she stocks. Birthlight advises a similar technique but adds yoga breathing to the stretching. Gowri also does a vaginal tendon and muscle (myofascial) release, which is a type of massage through an internal examination, a combination of Bowen technique and craniosacral treatment. This can help to reduce pelvic spasm and also help to allow the baby to engage into the pelvis. This is carried out in the third trimester, and although there is very little written about this type of management, it has been very helpful in Gowri's extensive experience of birth. The Bowen technique is a relaxing soft tissue remedial therapy, named after its innovator, Tom Bowen. The technique involves the therapist using fingers or thumbs to move over muscle, ligament, tendon and fascia in various parts of the body. Craniosacral treatment is an offshoot of osteopathy. A craniosacral therapy session involves the therapist placing their hands on the patient, allowing them to tune into what they call the craniosacral rhythm. The practitioner claims to gently work with the spine and the skull and its cranial sutures, diaphragms, and fascia. In this way, the restrictions of nerve passages are said to be eased, the movement of cerebrospinal fluid through the spinal cord is said to be optimised and misaligned bones are said to be restored to their proper position. Both techniques are complementary therapies that, from experience, induce profound mental and physical relaxation.

Hypnosis and its impact on emotions, pain and birthing is fairly well documented in both medical and literary circles. It can have a very potent effect on reducing fear and promoting relaxation in potentially difficult situations.[49] Natal hypnotherapy and hypnobirthing are the most popular birth hypnosis approaches in the United Kingdom. I used the Gentle Birth Method's self-hypnosis CD, which I found invaluably helpful and would definitely recommend to all my patients. Many other pregnant women including doctors that I met during this time said that birth self-hypnosis was the key therapy that helped them cope with natural birth.

There has been very little research into nutritional preparation of the tissues essential to labour, although the government provides plenty of advice on which foods are considered safe to consume during pregnancy. In 2010, The Royal College of Obstetricians and Gynaecologists issued advice warning pregnant women not to become obese in pregnancy by over-eating. I followed the advice given by the Gentle Birth Method, particularly because the Ayurvedic principles on which it is founded resonated with my Asian upbringing. My abdominal bloating, overall health and general appearance certainly improved by following

Gowri's nutritional advice. Again, I followed the recommendations of an experienced practitioner whom I trusted rather than sticking to conventional advice. If only more research could be funded in this area: food becomes flesh in the end, so when preparing the uterus and pelvic tissues for labour, we could do a lot more to improve the quality of our intake. Nutrition is therefore an important part of becoming birth fit. I was not familiar with the nutritional supplements suggested by Gowri, but I had faith in her expertise and was willing to try them. Ayurvedic herbs have a long and well-known history in India and Sri Lanka for their use in pregnancy, and the traditional western herbal tea combination of nettle, cramp bark, red raspberry leaf and squaw vine leaf is also known to detoxify and tone the uterus. In the end, my uterus behaved perfectly in labour, unlike the usual slow labours that I have seen in women over forty. I felt this nutritional advice revived my health, and my midwife Rachel was impressed by my reversal from poor to good health owing to my birth preparation tactics.

My mother arranged for me to listen to a chanting session of Buddhist Pirith blessings, a traditional ritual in Sri Lanka for the spiritual support of the mother and fetus. Buddhist practices have been carried out for thousands of years to promote equanimity in expectant and labouring mothers in order to improve the emotional outcome and spiritual potential of the baby. Listening to the Angulimala Sutta, a non-theistic chant, has long been considered a potent form of birth preparation and labour accompaniment, which helps to dispel the fear surrounding labour and birth, as well as mitigating physical and mental pain. I found it very touching to be in the presence of supportive relatives and family friends along with the Buddhist monk Venerable Bandula, all wishing me and the baby well. Nurturing cultural support such as this for pregnant women has been considerably diluted in modern society. However pregnancy yoga or active-birth groups provide a more contemporary circle of support, and there is gathering evidence that when women support each other it releases high quantities of natural oxytocin, which counteracts stress by subduing high cortisol levels. [50-52]

I was not sure what types of pain relief I would prefer in labour, so I ordered a TENS machine and a birth pool just in case. I stocked up on a waterproof sheet for my bed and a lot of protective home-decoration plastic sheeting. My midwives left me a stash of midwifery equipment such as absorbent pads, and I had a birth-ball to help me stay upright. Despite these home preparations, my hospital bag was packed, just in case of an emergency by 36 weeks. After the birth preparation had been done, I became very excited about the prospect of going into labour – I was eager to see how it would work for me. As with most of the women I had met who had similarly prepared, I had the courage and the acceptance to take on the experience without fear. Being at home and able to use my own bed, bathroom and environment, was going to be far more relaxing than being in hospital. I was confident that my body would work well if I just continued to relax, was in the present moment, felt well supported and was allowed to get into the misty, serene, uncrowded consciousness in a dimly lit room that is so beneficial for birthing. In Chinese medicine this is a very "yin" state of femininity. The day before I went into labour, I emailed Ina May Gaskin about my hopes for a homebirth:

> *The baby has been quite clever in keeping me away from my work as an obstetrician....I now know it was to truly de-programme me. I am looking forward to a homebirth any day now, which has caused a few raised eyebrows amongst my obstetric consultant colleagues, especially as I am 42 yrs. You know, it is very odd and rather lovely to be a mother making this decision and realising that, despite all the statistics that are present about risks surrounding birth, the most important factor is my innermost instinct that my body will behave much better if I can birth at home, and also the inner dialogue between mother and child, where the child clearly wants to be born at home. In fact, my little one makes me feel quite ill when I hang about my hospital too long...despite being surrounded by caring colleagues.*
>
> *I have not worked as an obstetrician since I was eight weeks pregnant when I had severe nausea and vomiting....I could not seem to cure it with all my best efforts as an acupuncturist and a homeopath or*

in fact any natural cure (I don't really take allopathic medicines). But now I realise that the baby was simply keeping me away from work...otherwise I would not de-programme myself or come to the conclusion that I would prefer a homebirth. I have cured so many women with nausea and vomiting in pregnancy with acupuncture...I was initially quite puzzled by it not working on me.

Ina May's response to me was:

How wise of your child to demand your full attention by making you too nauseous to continue work. I'm delighted that you'll be trying for a homebirth. We've had a few for primips of your age, and they did very well. The main challenge, I think, is how to get to the ape consciousness or monkey mind, if you prefer. Teenagers already usually live there, but it's a little more rare in women over 30 or so, who've had to become used to functioning in a world that is still mostly arranged by men.

Of course, the wonderful thing about love is that we can create more and more of that with our minds, words, and actions. To create it during labour, even if that hurts more than one has experienced so far, is the gauntlet some of us run to become mothers. I'll be keeping you in my heart and mind during the coming days, and I look forward to hearing the news of your birth – but not until you're ready to look outward again.

I regarded that as a blessing and that very night I went into labour, with my waters breaking at the height of a full moon.

THE BIRTH

On the evening before my waters broke, I spent my time watching videos of Ina May Gaskin, Michel Odent and Eckhart Tolle, which I found hugely inspiring. When my waters broke in bed at midnight with no contractions, I phoned Rachel and Kim to let them know. Rachel and I were so excited about it that we didn't manage to sleep at all after this – and it was only then that I realised both the birth pool and TENS machine I had ordered had not arrived. Luckily, Françoise, who I had also contacted, was holding a Birthlight course in London and kindly said that she would bring her demonstration birth pool in for me to borrow. All I had to do was arrange collection!

It was standard hospital practice, at the time I went into labour, for the mother to come to the hospital for an internal examination when her waters had broken. This involves the use of a speculum to check the colour of the water. Typically, the diagnosis is confirmed by the presence of a pool of fluid in the vagina after which the fetal heart is monitored with a cardiotocograph. With a homebirth the approach is much more low-tech: if the fluid is clear and the baby can be felt moving, the woman is reassured and asked to carry on as normal and wait for contractions to appear. That was the case with me and Rachel told me to try to cuddle up to my husband and get some sleep. The midwives would come to my home once the contractions started. My husband got busy waterproofing the house in the middle of the night and then we tried to sleep.

Tightenings started at 7am; by 9am, when both Rachel and Kim arrived, I was starting to contract more regularly. Kim examined me and found me to be 3cm dilated. From then on, Rachel stayed with me continuously until the birth. Kim went to the labour ward to get some more midwifery supplies, returning a few hours later. During this time I sat on my birthing ball in my sarong, continually rotating my hips and focusing deeply on my yoga breathing. It was all quite bearable: my mind was misty, my attention was internally directed and I felt at times that I was at the centre of a doughnut of time and space. Another consultant gynaecologist friend and her husband collected the birth pool for me and constructed it in my living room while I kept myself quietly in my own space in my bedroom. Rachel said that the sight of my husband and two friends setting up the pool was very comical to watch, rather like the Marx brothers, but somehow it all came together in the end. The pool was ready by mid-day and my friends quietly retreated. My husband, Rachel and Kim remained with me, calmly supporting me and protecting my birthing space. The midwives unobtrusively carried out their usual checks.

All this time, coping with the pain with yoga breathing was quite graceful. I took a dose of homeopathic Caullophylum 30C every hour, to help the efficiency of the contractions. At about 1pm, after going to the toilet, I had a very strong contraction and vomited. Rachel examined me and found that I was 5cm dilated and that the baby's head was below the half-way mark of the pelvis. The contractions then intensified. My husband attempted a little acupuncture on me but it stimulated the contractions even more and I found I just wanted to jump into the warm waters of the birth pool to cope with the discomfort. After about five minutes, I had him take the needles out and I got into the pool. Rachel and Kim raided my tupperware collection from the kitchen and used plastic boxes to pour the warm water over my back; the height of the pool water came to just below my breasts. By this time, the contractions were very strong, and I let them wash through me, aided by the yoga breathing and the warm water. Sitting in the pool was uncomfortable and I instinctively felt that it was better for me if I leaned forward on my knees, holding on to the sides of the pool. In this position, Françoise had taught me to make the "Ah" sound, which I did with each contraction. After an hour and a half I could feel a pressure down below and I instinctively examined myself to find out where the head of my baby was: it was only about 2cm from the outside world. I was obviously fully dilated and continued to keep breathing the baby out.

All was not completely straightforward, however: both of the fetal heart sonicaids that Rachel and Kim were using to listen to my baby's heart in between contractions had stopped working after half an hour, and although I was concentrating on my own inner space, I could see they were both worried about the equipment not working and had called the homebirth team to bring another one round to my house. Through our inner communication, I knew my baby was fine and I wanted to continue working on breathing him out but I could see the midwives were growing nervous about the risks. It was then that I expressed my only obstetrician thought in medical terminology: "I suppose I better expedite the delivery by pushing!" Three pushes later, my baby was born. My husband was waiting to cut the cord, but my baby snapped his own cord on his exit and was caught swiftly by Kim. He was then placed in my arms and Rachel remembers me saying spontaneously "I love you" to him, although I don't recall it myself. He looked so fragile, with intense eyes and sharp features, like a wise little fellow and an old soul.

I got out of the pool and into a warm bathrobe, and then sat on my couch and breastfed my baby to help release the placenta. I opted for a natural/physiological delivery of the placenta despite all my research into drugs that help this stage of labour, because I wanted all the benefits of having high levels of natural oxytocin. The placenta came out after an hour, an experience that, somehow, I felt was more painful than delivering my baby. I required a few stitches for a tear, which were expertly taken care of by Kim, and my blood loss was below average. The midwives and my husband tidied everything up and we were all snuggly at home as a family, with my parents nurturing us all with tea and cake. The homebirth was very simple, profound and empowering for me. This low-tech birth, achievable by most pregnant women, was one of my greatest accomplishments.

PART 2
THE THEATRE OF BIRTH

CHAPTER 3
THE PAIN OF EVE,
THE POWER OF THE GODDESS

I speak from my perspective as a woman born in Sri Lanka and an obstetrician educated in the United Kingdom. With a foothold in both worlds, I developed an image of womanhood drawn from both Eastern and Western culture. My curiosity as a scientist was defined by a sense of seeking mastery over nature, with wanting to fix and mend things. Yet my childhood training in Sri Lankan dance and drumming, combined with a strong influence from a mystic grandfather, bound me to the esoteric. As life unfolded, it was only through my own pregnancy that I uncovered how my own ideas of womanhood had been shaped by both influences. I realised how myths and religious stories still shape the ideas of society, despite science's bid to overthrow traditional beliefs.

Joseph Campbell, American scholar and mythologist,[53] proposed that myths and religious stories provide a psychological road map for the finding of oneself in the labyrinth of the complex modern world. The biblical story of Eve suffering painful childbirth because of the original sin of yielding to temptation is deeply embedded in the psyche of Western society, and the pain of childbirth is set as a kind of gold standard of the experience of a mother. Childbirth from this model is seen as a disempowering, unfair experience that the female gender has to suffer, and a modern-day woman, who has access to the latest medical technology, may feel that it is totally unnecessary to experience such

Marc Chagall, God Rebukes Eve.

A potent reminder of the Western archetype of the pains of childbirth.

South Indian wood carving, Kali Giving Birth.

An empowering Eastern archetype.

pain in labour and opt therefore for a caesarean section even where there is no medical necessity. However, from other mythological perspectives, the female is represented by a powerful goddess. The importance of her role in renewing society is given due recognition and childbirth is therefore seen in a more empowering light. From Ancient Egypt we know that there was a rich tradition of feminine divinity symbolised by Hathor/Sekhmet and Isis. These goddesses epitomised an empowered female; soft as well as dynamic and aggressive, giving pharaohs both vitality and life. Such female power governing the cycles of life, death and rebirth, is seen in many goddess myths and archetypes across the world.

The goddess, from a feminine perspective, represents a particular feminine archetype. This archetype, a concept at the heart of Carl Jung's psychological works,[54] is a deep, enduring pattern of thought and behaviour laid down in the human psyche, which remains powerful over long periods of time and transcends cultures. Archetypes form the basis of all unlearned, instinctive patterns of behaviour shared by humankind, regardless of culture. Archetypes are found in dreams, literature, art and myth, and are communicated to us through many symbols. Archetypes comprise the source of emotional symbols, which, in turn, attract energy, structure it and influence the creation of civilisation and culture. We underestimate how deeply myths shape health-seeking and healthcare delivery behaviour in our modern systems. Western medicine has been shaped by Western culture, and thus the alleviation of Eve's pain and suffering during childbirth is a philosophical and scientific priority. However, in powerful goddess societies such as South Asia, the priority lies in nurturing the mother during and after pregnancy, which imparts body confidence and enhances a woman's experience of birth. Gaining the feeling of empowerment that successful natural childbirth imparts is important; childbirth is a rite of passage for a woman to journey into greater feminine wisdom and maturity.

In my conversations at the Royal Society of Medicine with Dr Luke Zander, a retired British general practitioner who had been involved in 300 homebirths and who continued to look after the families and children for many years afterwards, I became intrigued by his panoramic view of birth. This type of longitudinal perspective on the mode of childbirth and its impact on the family – and therefore society as a whole – is not usually experienced by midwives or obstetricians because they look after pregnancy in an episodic way rather than having the opportunity to observe family life over a long period of time. Dr Zander explained the wider significance:

> *As a result of this, one inevitably becomes aware of the long-term effects, both positive and negative, of this very major experience, which in many instances can be exceedingly significant to the physical, psychosocial and emotional well-being of the mother. Because of the importance of this long-term effect, it always seemed to me that we should give very careful thought as to how we, as professionals, can do all we can to ensure that the experience of giving birth can be optimised.*

> *It was for this reason that I undertook a study of the "long term" (more than five years) birth memories of two cohorts of women giving birth at home or in hospital. It was an attempt to identify those qualitative factors that were bought out in the two groups; and the findings were very interesting and thought provoking. [55-58]*

> *The memories were very strong, and the accounts of the birth often sounded as if the event had happened very recently. So it is not something that slips into oblivion, and this needs to be recognised. The memories of those women who had been allowed/ encouraged to give birth at home, i.e., in the place of their choice, irrespective of whether or not they ultimately had to go into hospital, were universally positive, whereas those having a hospital birth almost always had some negative recollections, even if the overall response was positive.*

> *A very interesting difference between the two groups was that many of the women who had a birth at home made very positive comments relating to how it had affected them as individuals, how it had strengthened their own sense of themselves, which then led on to how they felt enhanced in their role as women, mothers and partners. This was rarely mentioned by the "hospital group", who instead felt positive about what had been done for them by their midwives and doctors.*

Dr Zander's experience gives us valuable insights into the effect of the birth experience and a woman's subsequent feelings about herself.

There is substantial evidence[59;60] that anxiety surrounding childbirth leads to long-term mental ill-health consequences in the mother. This is particularly linked to anxiety experienced in late pregnancy and the experience of delivery. Those who study this area have found that in pregnancy, depression, severe fear of childbirth, "pre"-traumatic stress, previous counselling related to pregnancy/childbirth, and self-reported previous psychological problems were associated with an increased risk of experiencing post-traumatic stress within one to eleven months postpartum. So a woman's ideas about childbirth influence how likely she is to develop post-traumatic stress disorder as much as any other independent factor such as physical trauma.

Aside from the images and myths that influence how we feel about birthing, Carl Jung's mother archetype is our in-built ability to recognise the relationship of "mothering" or being nurtured.[61] We have evolved in an environment that includes a mother or mother-substitute; we come into this world ready to want mother, to seek her, to recognise her, to deal with her. He says we project this archetype out into the world, typically onto our own mothers, but if the mother fails to satisfy the demands of the archetype, the individual may spend his or her life seeking comfort elsewhere: in the church, in identification with "the motherland", in a life at sea, or in meditating upon the mythological figure of the mother. Historically, during childbirth, women have relied upon the support of a motherly figure to help them through labour, which has become the midwife or the supportive figure of a doula. There is something about the presence of this archetype that aids a woman through the labour process and is a key ingredient in the promotion of normal birth. Today this concept has been translated into "continuous emotional support" (a term coined by the medical profession from research into this area) throughout labour, which leads to a proven reduction in pregnancy complications.[62] Before my pregnancy, I was aware of this in a very intellectual, academic way, but throughout my pregnancy I really connected with the validity of this and understood that, besides the technology of obstetrics, the key to developing the confidence to birth in a normal way, was found in the nurturing and mothering that I received from midwives and natural birth experts and through pregnancy yoga.

Natural childbirth promoters utilise positive birthing and mothering archetypal imagery to transform the fear of childbirth into confidence. It is a very powerful form of prenatal education that works deeply without engaging the rational mind. Throwing facts and figures at women undoubtedly helps them to understand their choices, but it is more important that women are guided to unlock confidence in their bodies to embrace the process of birth. Without this, an almost virulent form of fear can sabotage their innate capabilities to birth well, quite aside from any genuine medical issues. The media is rife with pregnancy disaster stories – which sell more papers – and doctors operate from the perspective of "worst case scenarios", because the majority of their work dwells on fixing problems in pregnancy. It is up to the midwives, doulas and natural-birth experts to provide an encouraging view of normal childbirth that affirms women's basic programmed potential to give birth. When a supportive network surrounds a woman, she has more opportunity to unlock her own innate inner birthing wisdom.

CHAPTER 4
GUARDIANS OF NORMAL BIRTH

THE MIDWIFE

Every day my respect for midwifery grows, particularly my respect for those midwives who have mastered the skill of eliciting normal birth, an art form that is acquired through apprenticeship and intuitive experience. I now understand that good midwives have a capacity to wait for nature, one that doctors, with their "fix-it" mentality, inherently do not have. This capacity for waiting produces a supportive force field around the labouring woman that allows her, in turn, to tap into her natural ability to birth. I did not fully grasp this when I was a young doctor and apologise unreservedly for my former view of midwives as more autonomous versions of nurses – a view that midwives, understandably, find very irritating in doctors.

It is helpful to realise that the word midwife comes from the Old English term "with woman", which reflects the midwife's role of waiting for nature and supporting a woman during pregnancy. The French term for midwife, "sage femme", or wise woman, is equally revealing. Throughout history and across all cultures there has been a tradition of women, most usually those with their own experience of birth, supporting other women during childbirth.

Pregnancy and birth are normal life processes and midwives are there to provide support and care during this time. The ethos of the midwifery model of care in Britain includes:

- Monitoring the physical, psychological, and social well-being of the mother throughout the childbearing cycle.
- Providing the mother with individualised education, counselling, and antenatal care, continuous hands-on assistance during labour and birth and postpartum support.
- Minimising technological interventions.
- Identifying and referring women who require obstetric attention.

Woman-centred care has been proven to reduce the incidence of birth injury, trauma and caesarean section. The Cochrane database, an electronic database that amalgamates the current scientific data of many different aspects of health, contains a current review of the benefits of midwifery care, as outlined below.

Midwife-led versus other models of care for childbearing women [63]

Midwife-led care confers benefits for pregnant women and their babies and is recommended.

In many parts of the world, midwives are the primary providers of care for childbearing women. Elsewhere it may be medical doctors or family physicians that have the main responsibility for care, or the responsibility may be shared. The underpinning philosophy of midwife-led care is normality and being cared for by a known and trusted midwife during labour. There is an emphasis on the natural ability of women to experience birth with minimum intervention. Some models of midwife-led care provide a service through a team of midwives sharing a caseload, often called "team" midwifery. Another model is "caseload midwifery", where the aim is to offer greater continuity of caregiver throughout the episode of care. Caseload midwifery aims to ensure that the woman receives all her care from one midwife or her/his practice partner. By contrast, medical-led models of care are where an obstetrician or family physician is primarily responsible for care. In shared-care models, responsibility is shared between different healthcare professionals.

The review of midwife-led care covered midwives providing care antenatally, during labour and postnatally. This was compared with models of medical-led care and shared care, and identified 11 trials, involving 12,276 women. Midwife-led care was associated with several benefits for mothers and babies and had no identified adverse effects. The main benefits were a reduced risk of losing a baby before 24 weeks and a reduced use of regional analgesia during labour, with fewer episiotomies or instrumental births. Midwife-led care increased the woman's chance of being cared for in labour by a midwife she had got to know. It also increased the chance of a spontaneous vaginal birth and initiation of breastfeeding. In addition, midwife-led care led to more women feeling that they were in control during labour. There was no difference in the risk of a mother losing her baby after 24 weeks. The review concluded that all women should be offered midwife-led models of care.

The midwifery and medical models for the care of pregnant women are based on separate perspectives of pregnancy and birth. These include differences in philosophy and focus in the relationship between the care provider and the pregnant woman; in the main focus on prenatal care; in the use of obstetric interventions and other aspects of care during labour; and in the goals and objectives of care. The midwifery model has advantages for many women because it avoids unnecessary interventions during labour thus helping the process remain normal, and because it addresses needs that are often not adequately met by the medical management model. Yet the delivery of care resulting from these two perspectives can be synergistic. As a result of midwives and physicians working together, there has been significant merging of the models. Instead of only two, completely separate, ways of managing birth, there is wide variation ranging from a totally integrated team, to mutually exclusive management teams.

In the United Kingdom, a midwife is legally obliged to attend births that she is notified of, but the law does not assert the same for an obstetrician. This means an obstetrician can refuse to attend a birth and someone else will have to take his or her place, whereas a midwife cannot. In pregnancies with medical complications, midwives play a supportive role, while doctors take on a more managerial/surgical role.

In an ideal world, the Department of Health in the UK would like:[64]

- Flexible, individualised services designed to fit around the woman and her baby's journey through pregnancy and motherhood, with emphasis on the needs of vulnerable and disadvantaged women.
- Women being supported and encouraged to have as normal a pregnancy and birth as possible, with medical interventions recommended to them only if they are of benefit to the woman or her baby.
- Midwifery and obstetric care being based on providing good clinical and psychological outcomes for the woman and baby, whilst putting equal emphasis on helping new parents to prepare for parenthood.

These recommendations are improving the care of pregnant women. In addition, there are governmental policies regarding choice of maternity care for women, which government hospitals strive to meet, and are a driver for change from the former traditional system. Despite these policies and even with massive efforts by dedicated staff, women's care within the current National Health Service system is inherently limited by finances, in that, a woman's care is determined by what enables the institution to function within a given budget. Options for maternity care are also hindered by the current shortage of midwives throughout the United Kingdom. A fundamental change in structure is required, which is being addressed by a recent government policy directive called "Maternity Matters",[65] indicating a commitment to developing a high-quality, safe and accessible maternity service through the introduction of a new national choice guarantee for women. This aims to ensure that all women will have a choice regarding the type of care that they receive, together with improved access to services and continuity of midwifery care and support. It remains to be seen how this policy will unfold.

Hospital midwives are used to working synergistically with doctors. It is noticeable that certain personalities are drawn particularly to hospital midwifery, community midwifery, homebirth teams and independent midwifery. Those who are drawn away from the hospital environment often have a different philosophical approach to those who work closely with doctors. The cultural milieu of hospital midwifery today is causing it to become more and more bureaucratic and a hospital environment, with its attendant duties, policies, risk-management criteria, protocols and larger volume of high-risk patients, is not an optimum environment for instinctual practice. Very broadly speaking, it depends where on the risk management/instinctual spectrum midwives feel most comfortable that governs the setting they are drawn to work in.

In the United Kingdom, independent midwives are private practitioners who work outside of the NHS and can provide women with a unique model of midwifery care that is very woman-centred. The fundamental and pivotal difference between this model and that provided within the NHS is that the woman chooses and pays for her midwife. From here flows a relationship of partnership between the woman and midwife in which individualised, responsive care is provided. This includes:

- Unhurried antenatal care, a crucial and integral part of the childbearing experience, which enables the woman to explore issues through full and thorough discussion and which leads to her making genuinely informed choices about her care. This process of decision-making enables the woman to gain confidence in her ability to birth and to parent positively and effectively.
- Labour care with the midwife, with whom a relationship of trust has developed throughout the pregnancy.
- Postnatal care and support for up to a month following the birth.

Independent midwives are aptly named: they almost do their best to avoid contact with the medical team, but if medical help is required they know how to access it. Independent midwives are in the minority in the United Kingdom but all midwives in Britain practice under the regulatory guideline of their professional body, the Nursing and Midwifery Council. All midwives offer a potential bridge between instinctual childbirth and scientific childbirth.

Midwifery is a strong and respected profession in the United Kingdom, and in the Netherlands it is more powerful still, but it is less so in terms of respectability and influence in the United States. Market forces and the battle for the bounty of delivery fees was curtailed by the inception of the National Health Service in Britain in 1948. In the United States however, where private healthcare delivery is the norm, the power of the midwifery profession was eroded during the twentieth century, losing the competition for the birth market to the medical profession, which expounded the view that hospital birth was the "safest" way to have a baby. Since the 1970s, however, there has been a slight revival in American midwifery under the influence of the natural childbirth movement. But market forces still retard its growth, which is currently swayed by the fee-paying structure of insurance companies and the domination of the medical profession. The American College of Obstetricians and Gynecologists has historically been against the concept of homebirth and there are noticeable political undercurrents regarding policy-making in this area, whereas the Royal College of Obstetricians and Gynaecologists in Britain has always supported homebirth as an option for low-risk mothers, and total midwifery care of uncomplicated pregnancies is seen as quite a normal practice.

Broadly speaking, in the United States, there are three types of midwives: certified nurse midwives (CNM), certified (direct entry) midwives and lay or empirical midwives. There is a degree of politicking among these three groups, which some believe has contributed to the demise of midwifery in the United States by isolating midwives from each other. In addition, individual states issue their own licenses outlining allowed midwifery practice, with wide variation between them. CNMs usually work from standing protocols that have been drawn up in conjunction with physicians. They can also obtain hospital admission privileges. Midwives without formal licences also practise and use herbs and complementary therapies in their work. They assist women at home and at birth centres, but some states bar them from attending homebirths.

In the United States, The Farm Midwifery Center in Summertown, Tennessee, is an unusual, noteworthy and successful midwifery practice, founded by world-renowned author/midwife Ina May Gaskin[66] and her midwifery colleagues. It was one of the first out-of-hospital birth centres in the country. This practice has had low rates of medical intervention with consistently good birth outcomes for nearly four decades. The statistics for this practice are impressive:

- Homebirth rate: 95.1%
- Non-emergency hospital transfer rate: 3.6%
- Emergency hospital transfer rate: 1.3%
- Vaginal birth rate: 98.6%
- Caesarean section rate: 1.4% (compared to the US average of 31.1%)

Ina May and The Farm midwifery team give care that enhances the physiological mechanisms of normal birth, probably due to one-to-one continuous emotional and physical care, which enhances endogenous oxytocin secretion.

Elsewhere, the Dutch model of midwifery is the strongest in the world, placing the natural character of pregnancy to the fore. Dutch midwives operate as autonomous high-status healthcare professionals. Alongside general practitioner physicians, they are responsible for all normal home and clinical deliveries. Their profession evolved differently to their counterparts in other European countries and in the United States. Since the beginning of the twentieth century, Dutch midwifery has been characterised by growing professionalism, improvement of qualifications and rigorous standards of recruitment and training, all the while maintaining the traditional low-tech style.[67,68] Midwifery in the Netherlands has always enjoyed a considerable amount of state support and even legislature to protect midwives against competition from doctors for normal deliveries, which has no doubt contributed to the fact that 75% of Dutch midwives are independent, and 34% of Dutch women give birth at home. Social attitudes also account for this, with birth considered more of a societal than a medical event.

So far the evidence from the Netherlands[69] suggests that for healthy women, home or hospital births are equally safe for the baby where there is the infrastructure to transfer the mother to hospital should the need arise. Midwives are trained in neonatal resuscitation, should a baby not breathe well after delivery, although this is rare. This is in marked contrast to the findings of the American College of Obstetricians, which, by pooling together lots of information,[70] concluded that homebirth is less safe for babies even though the actual risk is very small, although there has been criticism about the sources of their data. Essentially there does not seem to be any overall consensus[71-75] on perinatal safety because all of the information has been provided by observational studies which are prone to bias. Ethical considerations prevent us from conducting the randomised controlled trials that would lead to unbiased results. We will never be able to do an unbiased research study (randomised controlled trial) because it would be too ethically difficult to answer this particular question. The same group of studies also suggested that the medical intervention rate, operative delivery rate and associated risks to the mother were lower in planned homebirths of low-risk mothers.

In the developing world, the midwifery profession has generally less status than in the developed world. Midwifery training can vary from just a few months to become a skilled birth attendant, or more extensive training over a few years. Poorer countries are experiencing a brain drain of their most skilled midwives, who leave to seek their fortune in richer countries. The United Kingdom for example, eagerly absorbs the skills of midwives from overseas because of its own shortage of midwives. Due to high maternal and perinatal mortality rates in developing countries, the medical model of pregnancy tends to represent the ideal standard of maternity care. Access to adequate medical care is the central issue regarding mothers who die as a result of obstetric emergencies compounded by poverty, ill health, nutritional deprivation and low social status. The problem of maternal death in poor countries has been distilled into the concept of the "three delays" [76], i.e. delays in:

1. Identifying a pregnancy complication and deciding to seek appropriate medical care in an emergency.
2. Having the right family, societal and transport infrastructure to reach an appropriate obstetric facility.
3. Receiving adequate care at the facility.

So for these reasons, the major preoccupation of maternal healthcare providers in this situation is addressing the lack of access to medicine. So one can see how the ideals and values of holistic midwifery can be overpowered by medicalised concepts of birth.

In Sri Lanka, where I originate, the midwives perform an important public health role. They are not equivalent in skill levels to British midwives, but are trained for one year, recruited from rural towns and encouraged to stay within their original rural setting to ensure coverage of the healthcare system. In hospitals, pregnancy care follows a medical model and, here again, the midwives are aids to the medical system rather than practitioners in their own right. In Sri Lanka, homebirths are actually discouraged by the medical hierarchy due to anxiety relating to the first two potential delays mentioned above. Indeed, when there are limited healthcare resources, it makes sense to centralise services. In my experience, when in Sri Lanka for two months of my maternity leave, I found that my own stories about the wonderful experience I had of homebirth were frequently received with astonishment. The whole concept of the valuable role of the midwife in facilitating normal birth; of midwifery as a noble profession in its own right; of the majesty of normal childbirth and of a safe, healthy homebirth or delivery in a midwifery-led birthing centre was completely alien to those I spoke to, and was even considered by some as a sort of "first world luxury"! However, in much larger developing countries, where women travel great distances and over difficult terrain to reach hospitals, safer homebirth through skilled midwifery is an important contemporary issue. An internet search reveals the websites of holistic midwives from developing countries such as Senegal and Nepal,[77;78] who wish to improve the art of midwifery and offer patient-centred care. Whilst recognising the need for access to emergency obstetric services, these midwives seek to encourage the understanding that birth is usually normal, and not a medical pathology to be treated with drugs and surgery, except with rare complications. There is a significant art to facilitating normal birth that has been lost in the medical model of childbirth.

To summarise, international midwifery must confront the following:[79]

- The challenge of caring for a primarily healthy population within acute care facilities that focus on treatment of pathology.
- The challenge of helping women in rural settings with difficult terrain and inadequate transport links, and hence poor access to emergency obstetric care.
- The difficulty of predicting the individual nature of the experience and how childbirth will unfold.
- The importance of the continuous, attentive presence of caregivers and loved ones.
- The importance of respectful care of women and families – including clear communication, high-quality information and control over decision making – and of enabling their positive memories of the experience.
- Combating the incentives arising from private healthcare services, with their bundling and global fee-payment systems, which encourage use of interventions and measures to hasten and control childbirth, even though such care generally is not optimal for mothers and babies.
- Missed opportunities to prepare women to make informed decisions during their pregnancy and well before labour.
- The challenge for women, of making informed decisions about many crucial care matters while in labour and constraints on their choices at that time.
- The great extent to which services could be calibrated to provide more appropriate care, to increase benefit and to reduce harm and waste.
- Concerns about the severe impact of the malpractice system on maternity services.

There are now clear scientific and sociological benefits in support of the work of the midwifery profession. However, many governments of the world still do not invest financially, nor do they support midwives in their vital role in the care of normal pregnancy. Large-scale successful midwifery depends on governmental backing as seen in the British and Dutch examples of the profession.

THE DOULA

Within the current resource constraints of the UK's health service, it is not always possible to provide one midwife dedicated solely to each labouring woman. Essential medical monitoring takes priority and midwives are required to oscillate between two or more women in labour, making it extremely difficult to provide continuous emotional care during labour and childbirth. The figure of the doula has recently emerged to make up for this deficit in continuous emotional support. The term "doula" now refers to an experienced woman who offers emotional and practical support to a woman (or couple) before, during and after childbirth. The word originally stems from the Greek meaning "woman servant or caregiver". Doulas operate under the broad principle of mothering the mother, of enabling a woman to have the most satisfying and empowered experience possible during pregnancy, birth, and the early days as a new mother. Such support is of benefit to the whole family, helping them to relax and enjoy the experience.

There is a good research base stating the very positive advantages for using doulas during labour. As care of pregnant women becomes increasingly hospital based, resource restrictions have meant that midwives and doctors work in shifts, ensuring round-the-clock technical support, but a lack of continuity in emotional support. Doulas can provide the necessary emotional back up before, during and after labour. Doulas can also give advice on relaxation, breathing techniques, positioning and movement during labour. It is important to remember that a doula does not offer the specialised technical and healthcare expertise that a midwife provides, and is not a substitute for a midwife.

One of the first scientific research papers that showed the value of continuous emotional support in and above technical interventions, described in medical jargon as "active management of labour" was a study from Guatamala. The abstract is below.

Continuous emotional support during labor in a US hospital. A randomized controlled trial[80]

The continuous presence of a supportive companion (doula) during labor and delivery in two studies in Guatemala, shortened labor and reduced the need for cesarean section and other interventions. In a US hospital with modern obstetric practices, 412 healthy nulliparous women in labor were randomly assigned to a supported group (n = 212) that received the continuous support of a doula or an observed group (n = 200) that was monitored by an inconspicuous observer. Two hundred and four women were assigned to a control group after delivery. Continuous labor support significantly reduced the rate of cesarean section deliveries (supported group, 8%; observed group, 13%; and control group, 18%) and forceps deliveries. Epidural anesthesia for spontaneous vaginal deliveries varied across the three groups (supported group, 7.8%; observed group, 22.6%; and control group, 55.3%). Oxytocin use, duration of labor, prolonged infant hospitalization and maternal fever followed a similar pattern. The beneficial effects of labor support underscore the need for a review of current obstetric practices.

Since that study, more evidence has been gathered in support of these findings, and the Cochrane Database has now drawn from 16 further research studies to ratify these conclusions, as stated below.

Continuous support for women during childbirth[62]

Historically, women have been attended and supported by other women during labour and birth. However in many countries these days, as more women are giving birth in hospital rather than at home, continuous support during labour has become the exception rather than the norm. This has raised concerns about the consequent dehumanization of women's childbirth experiences. Modern obstetric care frequently subjects women to institutional routines, which may have adverse effects on the progress of labour. Supportive care during labour may involve emotional support, comfort measures, information and advocacy. These may enhance normal labour processes as well as women's feelings of control and competence, and thus reduce the need for obstetric intervention. The review of studies included 16 trials, from 11 countries, involving over 13,000 women in a wide range of settings and circumstances. Women who received continuous labour support were more likely to give birth "spontaneously", i.e. give birth with neither caesarean nor vacuum nor forceps. In addition, women were less likely to use pain medications, were more likely to be satisfied, and had slightly shorter labours. In general, labour support appeared to be more effective when it was provided by women who were not part of the hospital staff. It also appeared to be more effective when commenced early in labour. No adverse effects were identified.

It has also been found that psychosocial support by doulas has a positive effect on breastfeeding. So the benefits of simple human emotional support cannot be underestimated in the infrastructure of a medical birth setting. It clearly provides a key stepping-stone on the pathway to spontaneous normal delivery and improving the experience of childbirth.

There is more recent evidence in pure science, rather than medical journals, that the birthing hormone oxytocin, which fuels contractions, is released in higher concentrations when a person perceives love, trust and generosity from their surroundings.[81-84] Put simply, high levels of oxytocin lessen fear. This all adds to the overall picture that the humanistic aspect of care is possibly more influential in promoting normal birth than technocratic care. This is a humbling thought for an obstetrician.

There has been little research into the concept of improving pregnancy outcome by promoting "continuous emotional support" from sympathetic women as a low-tech intervention in poor areas of the world, where the first two delays are difficult to remedy because of poverty and terrain. It would be a difficult idea to test because of the lack of infrastructure in developing countries, especially in remote areas. However researchers have found that instigating a cascade of informal women's groups for socialisation, creating female networks and disseminating crucial health information has actually reduced neonatal mortality in rural Bangladesh.[85] Women chatting to each other and forming supportive networks could be a very powerful medium to encourage continuous emotional support for labouring women. Whenever I have worked in government hospitals in developing countries, I have noticed that the poorest patients were treated with very little privacy, dignity and sympathy by the majority of healthcare workers. Perhaps these prevalent attitudes can be overturned by a proliferation of supportive women's groups.

CHAPTER 5
HOW DOCTORS HELP AND HINDER

One of the strongest factors that inspired me to train as a doctor was the wish to alleviate the suffering of women in the developing world. When I was a child, I travelled overland by car from England to Sri Lanka, a journey that was to be a formative experience. My observations of womankind from varying cultures through the back windows of this car sowed the seeds that led me to become an obstetrician.

In the developing world, approximately half a million women die every year from problems related to childbirth, and I really wanted to help to reduce this humanitarian burden. Helping people overcome illness is a strong motivator for those who choose to study medicine, but in their attempts to deal with disease, doctors often lose sight of the normality of childbirth. The simplicity of childbirth, and a woman's innate ability to let her body use nature's programming to deliver a child – especially if a woman is well nurtured and nourished during her pregnancy – has, in most cases, been forgotten. Of course, if a woman has not been well nourished or nurtured, has a poor socio-economic status or has a pre-existing illness, as do large numbers of women in developing countries, then this sets them at a health disadvantage. For this reason, natural childbirth is quite a different entity in developed countries, as opposed to developing countries because of the baseline differences in health overall.

All models of health are also culture bound, even those based on science. Medical anthropologist and psychiatrist Arthur Kleinman points out:

> *Healing efficacy is not a straightforward resultant, but rather determined by evaluations which are tied to the beliefs and values of different sectors of healthcare systems, and which therefore might be (and often are) discrepant. Healing is viewed differently across cultures and in different sectors of healthcare. It is not the same thing for practitioner and patient. This is an argument to the effect that all healthcare explanatory models, including those of modern professional medicine and psychiatry, are culture-laden and freighted with particular social interests. And so is our present understanding of healing.*[86]

I used to believe that science offered absolute truths, but now, through my knowledge of epidemiology and statistics, I am aware of relativities and the politics of using science to interpret health. I remember my own prejudices against complementary and alternative therapies as a junior doctor, when it was the social norm to denigrate these other therapies, because as doctors, we only saw a skewed proportion of people with illness – those patients in whom such therapies have failed – and never saw the patients for whom they had worked well. Similarly, doctors in obstetrics mainly see problem pregnancies and never really experience the greater numbers of women who have normal pregnancies and non-medicalised births. Before my own homebirth, I had rarely witnessed the magical experience of an uncomplicated, low-tech delivery in a non-labour-ward setting. Because of this, obstetricians often feel that all pregnancies are potentially problematic until proven otherwise by a good outcome, whereas the midwifery principle is that most pregnancies are normal and only a minority of women encounter problems.

As a doctor, I have thought along the lines typical of my profession, but during my own pregnancy I became softer and very sensitive to the style of pregnancy care delivered to me. When I was in consultation with my own colleagues, I felt as though I could almost see the cartoon "thought" bubbles exuding from a medical consultation based on the principle of problem solving and problem prophylaxis. This is fairly understandable given the professional experiences of those involved, but nevertheless, this angle of service delivery, by its very problem-orientated nature, accentuates the word "problem", which understandably produces a degree of anxiety in the pregnant woman. Imposing too much risk-reduction strategy on a pregnant women can have consequences, which are divided into two main themes: objectification, including loss of control and an awareness of having a potential "risky body"; and exaggerated responsibility, including constant worry, continual pressure and even self-blame. I remember feeling slightly uneasy during my medical consultations as a pregnant woman, wondering what problem was going to be uncovered, whereas my midwifery consultations were wellness orientated and therefore very reassuring and anxiety-free. In the simplest and most telling terms, my blood pressure was always higher when measured by a doctor rather than a midwife – a clear, if perhaps surprising example of "white coat syndrome" in a medic! It was very interesting being on the other side of the fence.

Obstetricians have a peculiar role in medicine compared to other branches of expertise. Although they deal mainly with women with pregnancy-related illness, they also look after women who are well, so it is essential that they develop a bedside manner that allays anxiety in their patients rather than exudes the risk-reduction thought bubbles that suggest "Anything could go wrong at anytime.... I've got to do my best to stop it", and which are given away through body language. Of course doctors have to emanate an air of confidence to handle any medical complication that could arise so that the patient feels safe, but they should do this without evoking anxiety and being too paternalistic. This is a very fine balance that arises out of innate sensitivity and compassion or out of years of experience in dealing with humanity and perhaps being a patient themselves. I often feel that midwives understand the focus of care of doctors but that doctors don't quite understand the midwifery perspective. This again is probably because of the skewed proportion of ill patients that doctors manage, whereas midwives play a less influential role in the management of these women. Doctors are not always exposed to cases where midwives are able to demonstrate their prowess in the instinctual care of pregnant women.

If we provide an environment that is fearful, anxiety provoking and deeply suspicious of nature, one that we aim to command and control rather than to trust, then an inability to birth naturally becomes a self-fulfilling outcome in many of those who actually have the inherent ability to give birth. Medical healthcare seems blind to the effect that this type of risk-averse culture brings to pregnant women. It is undeniable that a medical safety-net is needed for those women who have medical problems, but there is room to improve the environment of birth to optimise their chances of normal delivery. The emotional state of women in pregnancy means that birth outcome is strongly linked to the continuity and quality of emotional support they receive. Midwives and doulas are better able to offer continuity than doctors who, obliged to look after many patients, can only reasonably offer intermittent presence/support throughout labour. There is no question that all women need access to obstetric emergency care, and here lies the benefit of obstetricians and of the medical system as a whole, but nevertheless, women are deeply sensitive to the attitude of their caregivers, and this should not be underestimated.

During my own, typical medical undergraduate education in the United Kingdom, students were required to be involved in 10 normal and 10 abnormal deliveries over an eight-week period. There was a lot of theoretical groundwork to cover and of course, as potential doctors who were motivated by altruism and/or the fascination of illness-related problem solving, we were more interested in the pathology or disease of childbirth than the normal deliveries. Thereafter during postgraduate education, there is so much to understand about disease processes and so much groundwork to cover to acquire technical surgical skills, that natural childbirth is not really part of the main medical focus. After my baby was born, I was surprised to find, during my own reading around childbirth activism,[87] that the Royal Free Hospital in London, one of the hospitals where I did some of my own postgraduate training, had been the site of recent activist controversy. In the 1980s, amidst objections from midwives, a woman called Nancy Hocking had attempted to give birth on her hands and knees instead of on her back, as was the current social norm. Hocking rallied a call to protest that was taken up by Sheila Kitzinger, who organised a protest rally on London's Hampstead Heath of 5,000 women carrying banners proclaiming "Stand and Deliver" or "Squatters Rights", which was instrumental in changing the practices of most British maternity units to accommodate natural childbirth ideas. Many years on, this event was never discussed in any postgraduate education that I received whilst working at that very hospital. There was nothing sinister in this, but childbirth pathology takes up so much of our time that there is no time to consider normal outcomes. Likewise, during conferences on obstetrics, there is very little discussion about natural childbirth or even the preventative health advantages of trying to reverse the tide of medicalised childbirth to keep it normal, healthy and free from intervention. It is well recognised that doctors across all specialities concentrate on finding and treating disease; there are many women alive today because of life-saving medical interventions, and that is what we work towards. But because of this, current natural childbirth issues do not filter into medical circles unless it is headline news or brought into the medical arena through government policy. However, political pressure through natural childbirth activists has worked its way into health policy in the United Kingdom, such as with the National Service Framework for Women, Children and Maternity Services.[64] Because of groups such as these, the whole climate of maternity care in Britain has changed considerably from the medical hegemony that existed 20 years ago. Although there is variation from centre to centre and there is still room for improvement, on the whole it is now much more flexible and patient centred.

Maternal mortality rates plummeted throughout the twentieth century in the United Kingdom. Although provision of better intrapartum (labour) care, emergency obstetrics services and antenatal care have contributed to these figures, they have not been as influential as the improvement in public health generally, owing to factors such as improved maternal nutrition, the advent of efficient blood-transfusion services, improved female literacy leading to empowerment and government investment in better social/agricultural infrastructure for the masses. In developing countries where less is spent on these factors, maternal mortality is still tragically high. The exception is Sri Lanka, where it is now well known that despite being a developing country it has achieved a very large reduction in maternal mortality because of coordinated medical services and its high levels of female literacy. Sri Lanka is an example to other developing countries of what can be achieved despite few available resources. However, in reducing maternal deaths through a medicalised model of birth, Sri Lanka has now started to see high caesarean-section rates of approximately 25% in the public sector and 70% in the private sector,[88] which is very similar to the situation in developed countries. It appears that, in emulating the western medical model, Sri Lanka has also acquired its flaws, providing another example of how the medical model of childbirth can overstretch and sabotage the normal birth process in the effort to increase safety.

The World Health Organisation has advised a caesarean section rate of 10-15%,[1] to provide a good balance between maternal and fetal safety. Statistics from The Farm Midwifery Center in Tennessee demonstrate that providing optimum environmental conditions for homebirth to a well-nourished, healthy community may reduce the caesarean-section rate to as low as 1.4%. Despite this, globally, the caesarean-section rate is rising:[89] in the United Kingdom it accounts for approximately 25% of all births, in the United States it is 31%, and in private practice worldwide it is notably higher. The leading drivers for the rise in caesarean sections are the existing medical culture and a preference for caesareans; the lack of the optimum environment to elicit normal birth in medical establishments; changes in obstetric training, loss of maternal body confidence and fear of labour; and a growing fashion in parts of Asia such as Hong Kong and Taiwan for wanting to secure the best birth timing to ensure an auspicious horoscope.[90;91]

Increasing the caesarean-section rate is not without its own health risks, which is why healthcare professionals in Britain are very concerned about this phenomenon.[92] These health risks may be immediate or longer term, and include the bio-behavioural consequences of the way we are born, which are more fully discussed in later chapters. So there is a delicate balance between maximising safety without increasing iatrogenic problems, that is to say, an illness which may inadvertently be caused by a doctor, a medical treatment or a diagnostic procedure. For instance, before the days of antisepsis and washing hands, puerperal or childbirth fever was an iatrogenic infection transmitted from one woman to another by their doctor. The Hungarian physician Ignaz Semmelweis made the connection in 1847 that doctors washing their hands between patients significantly reduced the number of deaths related to childbirth fever and subsequently developed theories concerning asepsis.[93] Nearly 100 years later, a similar correlation was observed in London, when it was noted that maternal deaths from puerperal fever were three times higher in London's Hampstead, where many women could afford to be attended by doctors or have babies in hospital, than they were in poverty-stricken Bermondsey, where women were attended by midwives at home.[94]

There is a view amongst natural-childbirth advocates that some obstetric interventions, if used for convenience – such as induction of labour, epidural anaesthesia and/or continuous fetal monitoring – unintentionally put women on a conveyor belt to medicalised birth, leading them away from the possibility of natural childbirth and all its benefits.[95] These benefits include the opportunity to experience the remarkable competence of birthing women and newborns, strengthen mother-baby bonds and foster a uniquely fulfilling and empowering experience, which, in turn, provides enormous social benefit to the mother-child dyad. The mother's surge of oxytocin at the time of birth stimulates loving feelings and is important both to the bonding process and in initiating breastfeeding. Medical interventions can interfere with the un-medicated and undisturbed infant's drive to crawl on its mother's chest, self-attach to the breast and begin suckling shortly after birth, which also provides the baby with a certain sense of empowerment in the social exchange of breastfeeding. During labour, the key beneficial effects of obstetrics are the availability of emergency obstetric services and the management of ill patients. However, there are many detrimental effects of obstetric "risk culture", such as reducing birth to a mechanical process devoid of understanding about the enormous bio-behavioural consequences of medicalised birth. This "risk culture", furthermore, has a negative impact on the mother's capacity to love, to bond and to breastfeed; on parent-child attachment and subsequent child rearing; on rates of psychological illness in mother and offspring; and on programming of adult health.[96,97]

In *A Guide to Effective Care in Pregnancy and Childbirth*,[98] Professor Murray Enkin et al suggest the code of practice to restrict unnecessary medical intervention in childbirth:

- That the only justification for practices that restrict a woman's autonomy, her freedom of choice and her access to her baby, would be clear evidence that these restrictive practices do more good than harm.
- That any interference with the natural process of pregnancy and childbirth should also be shown to do more good than harm.
- That the onus of proof rests on those who advocate any intervention that interferes with either of these principles.

Ideally, all decisions for medical interventions would be evidence based to ensure that treatments genuinely help patients. Doctors use research that falls under the broader umbrella term of epidemiology to establish what is a genuine effect of treatment rather than a random effect unattributed to the treatment or because of bias. (Epidemiology is defined as the study of the distribution and determinants of diseases and injuries in human populations. The very definition, once again, puts the focus on disease rather than wellness, although, equally, wellness could be extrapolated from the inverse relationship of illness.) The results of these research studies are then amalgamated and interpreted by policy makers to organise how health is delivered, concentrating on health interventions that bring about the maximum benefit for all. As a result of this, areas that have not been researched, due to lack of funds or simply because they are deemed unfashionable, tend to fall by the wayside.

The way in which research findings are interpreted can also be subject to politics. A conclusion that states "there is no evidence that a treatment works" can either mean that it has been tested and found to have no effect, or that it simply has not yet been assessed, i.e., the treatment may either have been proven not to work, or it has not yet been proven to work. In cases such as these, only historical information or expert opinion can advise the individual about the treatment in question. Some health professionals err on the side of caution when asked about a treatment that falls into this category, and instead of explaining that they simply do not know, they use the expression "no evidence" to warn patients against the treatment, perpetuating a misconception that it has been proven not to work. I raise this point because there are many aspects of natural childbirth care that are as yet unassessed scientifically, although there is traditional or historical knowledge available in support of their benefits. For this reason natural childbirth advocates can encounter resistance from the medical profession, which is governed by the need to minimise litigation.

It is important to note that some commonly used medical interventions have also not yet been proven to be beneficial. Electronic fetal monitoring (EFM) falls into this category. The current Cochrane meta-analysis of all research studies concludes that in comparison to using a fetal stethoscope intermittently to listen to the baby's heartbeat, there is little evidence of benefit to perinatal outcome. Conversely, there is evidence that EFM increases the rate of caesarean sections and instrumental vaginal deliveries, both of which have risks attached to them.[99] Nevertheless, if a baby were to come to harm or to perish prior to or during labour, the lack of an EFM record would mean that the hospital could not legally defend its standard of care, and so its use persists. Doctors argue that previous research studies may not have accounted for inadequate skill in the interpretation of EFM, or for failure to take appropriate action once abnormalities have been detected. As such, better mandatory training for staff may be advantageous.

Recently conducted research suggests that there are other interventions during labour and delivery that may inadvertently have a negative impact on long-term health, as summarised below:

Routine use of antibiotics
Babies exposed to antibiotics during the birth process were more likely than unexposed babies to experience persistent wheezing measured at six to seven years.[100] The initial colonisation of the newborn intestine with normal bacteria persists over a long period and has a pivotal effect on long-

term health.[101-103] Babies who experienced caesarean section, intrapartum antibiotics, hospital birth or who failed to breastfeed were less likely to have early colonisation with beneficial bacteria than those who were, respectively, born vaginally or at home, breastfed or not given antibiotics.[104]

Immune function

Babies born by normal labour as compared to those born by caesarean section have improved survival of white blood cells that destroy micro-organisms (neutrophils) in their cord blood and better neutrophil function. This suggests that labour may be immunologically beneficial to normal newborns and may help explain excess neonatal morbidity and mortality with planned cesareans.[105]

Long-term caesarean section complications

Caesarean section is associated with numerous adverse future harms in women, including abdominal adhesion formation, chronic pelvic pain, placenta previa, placenta accreta, placental abruption, uterine rupture and hysterectomy. Serious maternal morbidity increases progressively as the number of previous caesareans increases.[106-112] Babies born electively by caesarean section before 39 weeks' gestation have an increased risk of admission to neonatal intensive care units due to breathing difficulties, and death is more likely to occur.[113]

Ability to breastfeed and bond

Babies whose mothers received epidurals and/or systemic opioids during labour as compared to unmedicated babies exhibited reduced breast-seeking and breastfeeding behaviours, were less likely to breastfeed within 150 minutes of birth and cried more, whereas 90–100% of the unmedicated newborns exhibited all six measured breastfeeding behaviors.[114] Medical interventions decrease the likelihood of establishing breastfeeding.[96;97;115] The health risks to the child of not breastfeeding for six months are: [116-118]

- 40% more likely to develop type 1 diabetes.
- 25% more likely to be obese (in six months a formula-fed baby consumes 30,000 more calories than a breastfed baby).
- 60% more likely to suffer from recurrent ear infections.
- 30% more likely to develop leukaemia.
- 100% more likely to have diarrhoea.
- 250% likely to be hospitalised for respiratory infections such as asthma and pneumonia.

Opiates and adult drug addictions

Adults who met diagnostic criteria for drug addiction were about five times as likely as sibling controls to have received three or more doses of opioid and barbiturate drugs within 10 hours before birth.[119] When controlling for numerous potential confounders, researchers concluded that the association between pain medications and adult addiction appeared to have a dose-response effect. This was not found to be the case with drugs administered more than 10 hours before birth.[120]

Adult suicide risk

Men who committed suicide by violent means were about five times as likely as sibling controls to have experienced multiple trauma at birth (identified as events likely to cause pain to the baby). A sensitive window for effects ("imprinting") is postulated as the mechanism.[121]

Epidemiologically backed interventions tend to be applied in a type of "herd" approach to medicine rather than tailoring treatment to individuals. However, in the current climate, the health philosophy of patient-centred (individualised) care actually competes with evidence-based medicine protocols for the masses. Both philosophies seem to be at play in British health policy at the present time. Recent advances in the field of genetic epidemiology show that there is genetic variation in how we handle drugs or in predisposition to illness. For instance, some people respond to and handle drugs very well, whilst others using the very same drug may experience a side effect. Thus "protocolised" medical practice giving the same treatment to all patients with a specific problem may not be advantageous to a proportion of patients. Consequently, "herd" medicine will have to evolve to become more personalised, suggesting that, ultimately, there are forces within science heading to a personalised perspective to health.

CHAPTER 6
BIRTH ACTIVISTS AND THERAPIES
THAT PAVE THE WAY TO NATURAL BIRTH

In this chapter I shall discuss the views of some natural-birth gurus that captivated my attention, as well as complementary medicine therapies that can aid natural birth. There are, of course, many other natural-birth experts doing excellent work, but this book does not have the scope to discuss them all.

BIRTH GURUS

Gowri Motha and the Gentle Birth Method

Gowri Motha was born in Sri Lanka to Indian parents who have had a huge impact on the way in which she interprets health. Her father was a doctor and provided the necessary stimulus for her to undertake medical training, but her family's way of handling health with complementary therapies has had a lasting influence on the resources she has used to treat illness. This includes the use of Ayruveda, the "science of life", a very popular medical option for people in India and Sri Lanka. She trained to be a doctor in India and was an obstetrician in London for 12 years before moving her career laterally to a holistic way of managing conception, pregnancy, childbirth and the child's first year. She has called her practice "Gentle Birth Method, the Jeyarani Way", after her mother, Jeyarani.

Through her many years of experience as an obstetrician, Gowri came to the conclusion that much medical practice focused on the crisis management of labour. There was so little emphasis placed on preparing women emotionally and physically for labour and that many struggled to give birth and were ill equipped to cope with its demands, resulting in shock and unhappiness regarding their birthing experiences. Gowri also noticed that women in the developed world seemed to be giving birth to ever-larger infants, which adds to the potential mechanical problems that can be encountered, thus specifically inviting medical interventions such as caesareans and other instrumental deliveries when the baby fails to make its passage into the world. With these factors in mind she developed her method, crossing laterally from conventional medicine, and drawing from her own knowledge of complementary medicine and the Asian ethos of mothering the mother.

Much of her method is based on her own experience and is not yet based on scientific research. However, the birth statistics of the women undergoing her programme are much better than conventional obstetric care. Gowri's hands-on practice, with its many team members, is very busy and would probably welcome researchers to assess its effectiveness. However, there are so many areas of allied birthing practice that require investment of research time and funds that realistically it will be a long time before there are any research findings published in this area. This does not mean that Gowri's method doesn't work.

Her method is based on aiding the mother to prepare physically and emotionally for birth. For physical preparation, the method includes Ayruvedic dietary advice tailored to body type; the use of herbs, nutritional supplements and oils prepare the soft tissues of the body for birth; exercise advice and yoga. The emotional-preparation strategies comprise nurturing the mother, encouraging self-knowledge, confidence building, self-hypnosis and visualisations. The aim of the programme is to get the mother "birthfit" and thus able to meet the challenges of labour with confidence.

Françoise Barbira Freedman and the Birthlight Trust

Françoise Barbira Freedman is a medical anthropologist and pregnancy yoga expert. She is the founder of the Birthlight Trust, an educational charity offering a holistic approach to pregnancy, birth and babyhood, using yoga and breathing methods to improve the wellbeing of mothers and babies. Aqua yoga and infant aquatics is also part of her teaching ethos. Françoise spent a considerable amount of time carrying out anthropological fieldwork in Peruvian Amazonia, where she learnt about the area's gentle approach to parenting. She combined this knowledge with her expertise as a yoga teacher to develop an innovative programme of movements and nurturing relaxation for both mothers-to-be and new mothers and their babies. The Birthlight Trust has trained over 1,000 certified instructors in its four major teaching areas, mainly in the United Kingdom. The charity has also developed an international training programme and aspires to train midwives in its techniques.

"Birthing lightly" is a term often used by Françoise to describe her ethos. It is about giving birth without unnecessary strain, resistance or fear, and about feeling fit and strong in order to ease the baby's journey from the womb to the world outside. "Light" also refers to the potential esoteric aspect of using yoga for relaxed birthing.

Yoga can help to prepare a mother for birth and motherhood both physically and emotionally. Yogic breathing, for example, connects the action of voluntary and involuntary muscles in the abdomen. It does not involve an active use of memory, as it stimulates a deeper level of innate body wisdom that operates at a subconscious level, which the body remembers; yoga breathing helps the body remember how to help itself. By expanding both their breathing and stretching capacity, women gain greater confidence and control through familiarity with the muscles used in birth. Becoming more confident with their bodies and their ability to cope with labour mitigates birth anxiety. It should be remembered that pregnancy yoga is far gentler than non-pregnancy yoga. Vigorous forms of yoga such as Ashtanga can in fact be harmful in pregnancy and actually make it more difficult to give birth vaginally because of excessive pelvic floor tone.

Even for women with no prior experience of yoga, a few pregnancy yoga classes can reap significant benefits in helping to make the birth experience less traumatic. In contrast to approaches to "natural" or "active" childbirth, the main focus in pregnancy yoga is not the birth, but the woman's health and contentment as her body changes throughout the various stages of pregnancy, birth and postnatally. As the pregnancy advances, yoga is used to strengthen, tone, make space for the baby and aid relaxation.

Yoga can empower all stages of pregnancy, even in those cases of true emergency where intervention is necessary. Women who have prepared with yoga, find that their experience may be surprisingly fulfilling and their recovery considerably eased. Women who planned caesarean sections require much lower dosages of pain relief if practising relaxation before going into theatre, and their fitness after the birth often surprises health professionals.

Janet Balaskas and the Active Birth Movement

Janet Balaskas's teaching focuses on female empowerment. It encourages women to understand the process of labour and to see it not as a source of fear but as an amazing experience of life and an opportunity for human growth. Janet's method seeks to help women connect to the Earth and Gaia forces in the ground, to embrace the process, rather than think, "Oh my goodness, its going to be terribly painful and difficult. I haven't got the courage to face it. Perhaps the doctors can rescue me with an epidural as a first resort." Her approach turns women into active participants of the process rather than incapacitated recipients of care. Janet does not preach against medical intervention, because it is necessary for emergencies and for when a woman's personal reserve has been exhausted, but she coaches women to have a very positive and strong attitude towards the process, and to understand the benefits of a wide range of non-medical tools to improve the experience and efficiency of labour. She teaches yoga, breathing, relaxation techniques, using water for pain relief or birthing, and useful labour postures. Women who have attended her sessions say she has the ability to bring out the strength of a lioness in them and to help them to rejoice in their mammalian nature.

An active birth is one in which a woman is in control of her body, following her instincts and the natural physiology of normal labour and birth. She actively engages in the birth of her baby rather than being a submissive recipient of routine care. This will probably mean that she will move around freely, choosing comfortable, upright positions during contractions, and resting and relaxing in-between.

To aid this active birth process, Janet speaks of the benefits of weekly yoga classes where women sit in a circle and reconnect with the cultural roots of mothering. In this environment women learn from each other, quietening their minds and learning experientially from their bodies.

Yehudi Gordon

Yehudi Gordon is an obstetrician and gynaecologist, and a proponent of natural birth. The author of several books, he is one of the pioneers of the Active Birth Movement. He uses standard medicine and works synergistically with a team of allied professionals to optimise the chances of natural birth. He works alongside midwives, complementary medicine therapists, the Gentle Birth Method team, psychotherapists and counsellors to optimise the chances of natural birth. Yehudi is a keen advocate of the use of birth pools to ease labour. He embraced the concept of birth centres early in their evolution and believes in holistic women's health, founding the Viveka Centre in London, which offers an integrated approach to healthcare.

Michel Odent

French obstetrician Michel Odent was the head of the maternity unit in Pithiviers Hospital in France from 1962–85. One of the first obstetricians to introduce water births to western childbirth practices and to create home-like birthing rooms in the hospital setting, he is a prolific writer and speaker on the subject of the emotional and physical environment of birth, and how the birth environment has far-reaching effects on the emotional and physical attributes of adults. Since leaving the hospital setting, he continues to practise homebirth.

Michel Odent has several research publications in peer-reviewed scientific journals and has founded the Primal Health Research Centre in London. This research organisation holds a large database of cross-disciplinary research – animal, clinical studies and basic science – pertaining to the long-term consequences of early experiences. An examination of the Primal Health Research data bank[122] reveals a growing body of work indicating that health is, to a great extent, shaped during the primal period, i.e., from conception until the first birthday. It also suggests that the way we are born has long-term consequences in terms of our sociability, levels of aggression or, inversely speaking, our capacity to love.

In his exploration of the science behind the development of the human capacity to love, he has shown that oxytocin is not only responsible for causing womb contractions, but may also have a key effect on the physiological pathways of nurturing behaviour, feelings related to orgasms in sexual intercourse and the feeling of trust between people. He says that in order to give birth, mammals have been programmed to release a complex cocktail of behaviourally linked hormones during sexual intercourse, pregnancy, parturition and lactation. If the natural process is interfered with, without any clear medical advantage, such as life-threatening emergencies, then it may thwart certain aspects of human emotional development, but this can be investigated only through long-term studies.

Ina May Gaskin

Ina May Gaskin is a visionary midwife and birth activist. She is a marvellous public speaker and charismatic storyteller, enchanting her listeners with stories of her midwifery experiences and philosophy, all imparted with a wry sense of humour.

Spiritual Midwifery[123] is the most well known of her publications. In 1971, Ina May Gaskin and her husband Stephen founded The Farm, a self-sufficient eco-friendly community in Tennessee, where women gave birth in the settlement rather than in hospital, using the help of other women who lived there. It was through such hands-on experience that Ina May learnt the art of midwifery, founding a midwifery magazine, *The Birth Gazette*, and which led her to be known in the United States as the "mother of midwifery".

Her groundbreaking work *Spiritual Midwifery* presented pregnancy, childbirth and breastfeeding from a fresh, natural and spiritual perspective, rather than from the standard clinical viewpoint. The Farm Midwifery Center was set up 25 years ago, and The Farm midwives address the physical, emotional, spiritual, sexual and cultural aspects of their pregnant women. They believe that childbearing is a significant event for every family and that every mother has the right to a safe and satisfying experience.

One important element of Ina May's teaching is the promotion of natural birth and the knowledge that women's bodies are well equipped to give birth, as opposed to the risk-orientated view of childbirth that is fostered by conventional medicine. With the risk-orientated approach she says, "Ignorance of the capacities of women's bodies can flourish and quickly spread into popular culture",[124] leading healthy, fit women into the path of medicalised birth when there isn't any medical need. Women delivering at The Farm Midwifery Center have a 98.6% chance of a vaginal birth and a 1.4% chance of a caesarean section, with 95.1% births completed at home.

Ina May has also published an article on the "Gaskin Manoeuvre",[125] a technique to overcome shoulder dystocia by putting the woman onto all fours. She keeps herself up-to-date on birth research and statistics and holds a national maternal mortality register because there is no other official register kept in the United States, unlike Britain, which holds a triennial confidential enquiry into all maternal deaths.[126]

Frederick Leboyer and Birth Without Violence

Frederick LeBoyer, a French obstetrician born in France in 1918, is a revolutionary medical commentator on the circumstances of birth and its long-term impact on the way in which we embrace and interpret life. His keynote book, *Birth Without Violence*,[127] was written in 1975 when the medicalisation of childbirth was possibly at its peak of influence and the power of midwifery at its lowest ebb. At this time it was the norm for birth to take place in a sterile hospital room, for caregivers to wear masks and for the baby to be hung upside-down after birth, slapped to make it breathe and then almost immediately afterwards taken from its mother to the nursery to be bottle fed.

The heart of the book focuses on improving the quality of the baby's birth experience. LeBoyer's message is that a sensitive, unobtrusive style of care that is deeply respectful of the natural process, as well as a peaceful atmosphere at the time of birth, helps the baby to be born with a minimum of emotional and physical trauma. A quiet and peaceful environment during labour is most important, as constantly distracting the mother from her inner space prevents her entering her timeless zone from where the best of her body's physiological functions operate. LeBoyer also advocated immersing the baby in a warm bath after delivery to ease the transition from the womb to the outside world.

LeBoyer had been head consultant (Chef de Clinique) in Paris during the 1950s, but after undergoing psychoanalysis he began to develop new ideas about the process of birth. He effectively moved from the paradigm of childbirth as a reflection of the pain of Eve suffering for her sins, to the paradigm of the powerful goddess. During frequent visits to India, LeBoyer developed a keen interest in yoga and its applications, particularly breathing and sound, for pregnant women and new mothers. He also developed insight into the benefits of infant massage by their mothers, the findings of which appear in his book *Loving Hands*.[128] There is now scientific corroboration for his ideas, such as the benefits of infant massage on child neurodevelopment.[129] Through his publications, LeBoyer has been hugely influential in promoting the benefits of natural birth and reclaiming the natural process from the previous hegemony of medicalised birth.

Joseph Chilton Pearce

Author and commentator on child development and subsequent adult emotional development, Joseph Chilton Pearce is a well-known and exceptional public speaker on human intelligence, creativity and learning. Part scholar, part scientist, part mystic and part itinerant teacher, Chilton Pearce's interest in natural birth grew from his opinion that many child development issues stem from the neurocardiological foundations laid in fetal life, a view that led him to become a natural-birth activist.

Chilton Pearce teaches that:

> *The crux of the issue of education is that there are only two types of learning; one is true learning and the other is conditioning. Conditioning is a fear-filled response by the older, or what we call the "hind" or "reptilian" brain. This is the reflexive, survival, maintenance brain that responds as if threatened. A form of learning does take place here, but it's conditioned learning and is intimately associated with the emotional states of hostility, anger and anxiety. If you want true learning, learning that involves the higher frontal lobes – the intellectual, creative brain – then again, the emotional environment must be positive and supportive. This is because at the first sign of anxiety the brain shifts its functions from the high, prefrontal lobes to the old defences of the reptilian brain.*[130]

Chilton Pearce cites US neuroscientist and psychiatrist Paul Maclean's neuroscience work, which suggests that the mother's emotional state during pregnancy determines the direction such an evolution takes within her developing fetus.[131] Her state of well-being determines whether fetal brain development concentrates on the frontal lobes or the ancient "reptilian" brain involved in survival. Chilton Pearce argues that a woman's pregnancy and birth should be as gentle as possible, to promote the optimal natural psychobiological development of her baby. According to Chilton Pearce, if a pregnant woman is entrenched in an environment that is not wellness-orientated and does not nurture her and the baby, then the resulting stress chemicals will cause more fetal hind-brain development, which will lead survival emotional behaviour such as anxiety and/or hostility to predominate in the child's development. Chilton Pearce says there is neurocardiological evidence that the heart is not just responsible for cardiovascular function, but that it also has a significant neurological and endocrinological role. He claims that there are neuronal connections between the heart and the limbic structure, which is the part of the brain enabling us to experience emotions. The heart also has an electromagnetic field through which the mother and child influence each other. Hence, the emotional quality of pregnancy and the birth experience can have an impact on the child's development.

THERAPIES THAT PAVE THE WAY

Many complementary therapies for pregnancy have not been assessed scientifically, but there is much that remains unassessed in standard medicine, too. My philosophy is that if there is a therapy that can help and my patients recommend it I will always explore it. Even if there is no scientifically plausible mechanism of action currently, paradigms change over time and explanations may arise in the future. The majority of doctors do not share this attitude, but I have certainly met more than a few medics who continue to be open minded, particularly with respect to their own health.

During pregnancy, expectant women and their doctors are keen to avoid unnecessary drugs, not knowing what effect they may have on the baby. Because of this, therapies that ease the discomforts of pregnancy without resorting to drugs are attractive to many women. Not all complementary therapies are without scientific basis: there is scientific evidence to suggest that both acupuncture and hypnotherapy shorten labour, reduce the amount of drugs or epidural that women require and promote normal vaginal birth.[132] Acupuncture has also been shown to be beneficial specifically for nausea and vomiting and muscular or skeletal pain.[133-135]

Some traditional herbs may be beneficial, such as ginger (for nausea) and red raspberry leaf tea (for preparation to labour) and they seem to be safe in pregnancy, although there is very little scientific documentation backing this.[136] Blue cohosh, a herb used to increase contractions or start labour, should be used with caution, as there have been three potential cases of adverse reaction.[137] But it must be remembered that herbs, although natural, are medicines when used for medical purposes, so I only take them under the guidance of experienced practitioners. Throughout my pregnancy I took an herbal tea to detoxify and prepare my womb for labour. It consisted of nettle, red raspberry leaf, squaw vine and cramp bark and was based on traditional knowledge, although there is no published scientific evidence for its efficacy.

In terms of other therapies, there is some preliminary evidence to show the benefits of following a prenatal yoga course during pregnancy, particularly on the woman's heart rate, autonomic adaptation responses, physical pain, stress and trait anxiety. Therapeutic touch has been found to have enormous benefit in all avenues of health, especially in the perception of pain.[138-141] For this reason it is very hard to disentangle how much aromatherapy[142] helps in and above massage or touch during childbirth from the studies available. From the existing research, it appears it is unlikely to have the same effect as acupuncture or hypnotherapy.

There is a paucity of research published on homeopathy, shiatsu, craniosacral therapy, reflexology, osteopathy, chiropractic, pilates and Bowen therapy and their health benefits, but they remain very popular therapies in those women seeking "drug free" alternative healing treatments during their pregnancy, and indeed, the Gentle Birth Method incorporates several therapies into its programme, which work synergistically for birth preparation. Many of my patients have told me of situations in which these methods worked for them when standard medicine had very little to offer, particularly for the so-called minor symptoms of pregnancy (e.g. backache or haemorrhoids) which actually constitute a major discomfort for women. I have witnessed quite startling changes in mood, alleviation of anxiety and raised confidence in women taking very simple treatments such as Rescue Remedy, part of the Bach Flower Remedy range, which I myself found tremendously beneficial in pregnancy.

Ideally, funds would be invested to assess the effects of these therapies in pregnancy, but as it is currently not a fashionable area to research in the scientific community, we continue to wait for evidence. Standard medicine will always be cautious about making any recommendations about these therapies until some evidence is present or there is more undergraduate and postgraduate medical education on other forms or traditions of medicine. Even though there are many treatments in obstetrics that do not have rigorous scientific evaluation (e.g. manoeuvres we use in the life-threatening emergency of shoulder dystocia, single- versus double-layer closure of the uterus at caesarean section, cervical cerclage, routine use of prophylactic antibiotic with rupture membranes at full-term, etc.), familiarity with the practice and the opinion of experts in the field ensures their continued use.

Reflexology with Gowri.

PART 3
EMPOWERMENT OF THE INDIVIDUAL AND THE COLLECTIVE

CHAPTER 7
INNER WISDOM

In this chapter, I will discuss how pregnancy provides a unique period in which the physiological changes in health can aid self-development. It is a special time that, if allowed to unravel its gifts, can help a woman to access right-brain activity, leading to significant advances in consciousness, such as overcoming primordial fears and reaching new levels of confidence in life. A woman can overturn the "shadow" – i.e., fearful or emotional – elements lurking in her consciousness and, having transformed them, arrive at a victorious state of being.

This concept has parallels with the goddess archetype in Jungian psychology. The goddesses of ancient times contained within them qualities of light and dark, nurturer and destroyer; opposing elements that we all posses. In Taoism, it is said that the outer sphere of life reflects or plays out that which we have internally. As we increase our awareness of these shadow aspects within our own psyche, we are less and less obliged to experience these difficulties through other people or outer circumstances. Furthermore, when acknowledged, these shadow parts, which we have initially resisted, become the most illuminating and transformative aspects in our lives.

Françoise Barbira Freedman subscribes to this idea, arguing that pregnancy is a time of unusual opportunity for women who have undergone earlier traumas, to heal their lives as they release their inner joy in preparing for their babies to be born.[143] At this period of time yoga teaches – perhaps more easily than at other times – the power of undoing resistance and allowing inner strength to come to the fore.

Further support is given by anthropologist Robbie Davis-Floyd, who says:

> *Rapid psychological growth and change in pregnancy are possible as they are not in usual structured life. Psychologists have noted the ease and speed with which pregnant women can benefit from psychotherapeutic techniques, for the near constant inner and outer flux of pregnancy keeps category systems of pregnant women in a continuous state of upheaval as old ways of thinking change to include new life. For example, growing a baby puts a woman in much closer touch with her own childhood experiences, allowing old, deeply buried thoughts and emotions to surface. Hopes and fears from the past and for the future merge at the surface of her daily consciousness, as time compresses in the physical experience of pregnancy, and past, present, and future together are carried in her womb.*[143]

It is my belief that pregnancy is a time when it is possible to heal not only the darker aspects of oneself, but also the ancestral patterns caught in our systems. The baby's personality or will-power in trying to get the attention of his or her mother can also be another factor in how the pregnancy proceeds. In my own experience as a busy obstetrician, being pregnant and overwhelmed by circumstances forced me to be still and happy with living in the moment. I believe my baby orchestrated events to enable him to birth in the manner that he saw was preferable. Through this experience I realised that some – although not all – babies exert their will strongly before birth and are far from being passive, floating beings accepting of any environment their mother provides. The only way that I could cope was to allow the pregnancy process to soften me emotionally and physically, to allow a strong being to reside within me. In that softening and stilling experience I discovered my own inner wisdom. My right-brain activity started to dominate, allowing me to access greater inner peace and information in the gaps between my thoughts. Perhaps it was the gradient of change from a very strong intellectual life to a very instinctual phase that made me become aware of the consciousness changes that prompted me to write this book. I feel that it is really this part of the brain that holds the key to successful birthing; tellingly, this is the part that is missing in the more modern, mechanistic model of pregnancy care that tends to be the norm today.

During my pregnancy I watched an online video[144] of neuroanatomist Dr Jill Bolte Taylor, who talked about her insights into the working of consciousness whilst she experienced a brain haemorrhage. There were strange parallels between a neuroanatomist having a stroke and an obstetrician having a baby: both situations provided the scientist with the opportunity to examine, from personal experience, the condition that she had studied for many years from a theoretical perspective. Dr Taylor's book, *My Stroke of Insight,*[145] is fascinating and led me to realise that my brain had experienced a similar transformation, but from a different angle. Dr Taylor's fascination with her experience was similar to my interest in the consciousness changes that occurred within me during my pregnancy. I don't think my experience of right-brain activity in pregnancy was as profound as her journey, but the key to the temporary portal into this type of brain activity lies in the pregnancy state. The characteristics of right-brain activity that she described are very similar to those experienced by birthing women when they access their inner wisdom.

The human brain has two hemispheres, described as right and left sides. They process the information of our experience of life in very different ways. The left "brain" acts like a serial processor; it handles logic, language and numbers. It gives us our identity, as someone separate from others. It handles our experiences in the past and our future possibilities. Scientific thought stems from this hemisphere, which processes statistics and risk-assessment of our environment. Although aggression does not necessarily arise from the left brain, the feeling of other people being separate and apart from oneself – as opposed to the feeling that we are all interconnected and part of a greater phenomena of all that manifests in the universe – is the foundation from which fear, intolerance for others and hostility arises.

The right-brain hemisphere acts as a parallel processer, appreciating information through the present moment. It is from where intuition, a feeling of inner peace, an absence of mundane brain chatter, a sense of interconnectivity with humanity and all natural phenomena stem, and from where a sense of inner wisdom arises. In modern society there is a definite bias towards left-brain activity, with right-brain activity seeming to have been relegated to those who pursue artistic, charitable or esoteric pursuits or ideas. However, to thrive in the world we need a balance of both sides: to dwell too much on left-brain processes results in feelings of isolation and anxiety.

To access a woman's physiological best during birth, I believe she must get into that "no-thinking zone" governed by the right brain. She must be in the present moment, not reminded of the past or strategising about the future. This is the state where natural endorphins are highest, and can help women to cope with birth pain. It was only after childbirth that I discovered a very poetic passage by Frederick LeBoyer on this state of being:[127]

> *In the past, in our memories.*
> *In the future, in our plans.*
> *We're always looking back, at what is gone,*
> *or ahead, at what is yet to happen.*
> *Never focusing on "here and now!"*
> *Yet if we have any hope of rediscovering the newborn*
> *baby,*
> *we must step outside of our own furiously running time.*
> *Which seems impossible.*
> *How can we step out of time?*
> *How can we escape its fast and furious flow?*
> *The only way is by trying to be fully with the present*
> *moment.*
> *Yes, to be here and now, as if there were no yesterday, no*
> *tomorrow.*
> *To allow any thought that the moment*
> *will end, that another appointment awaits,*
> *is enough to break the spell.*

As usual, everything is very simple.
And apparently impossible.
How can we reconcile the irreconcilable?
How can finite combine with infinite?
It can only happen if we open completely to the other,
which means completely forgetting oneself.

Pregnancy hormones soften the brain and body and allow right-brain activity to dominate. If a woman is nurtured during her pregnancy and allowed to surrender to this state, her whole body will act better during labour. Although medicine can help some women, it also hinders this particular opportunity; because of its risk-reductive approach to childbirth it keeps women in a left-brain state of mind. I was pummelled into this right-brain state by the circumstances of my own pregnancy, which kept me away from work. This prolonged absence effectively deprogrammed the "obstetric" frame of mind out of me. But of course, I also knew where to find the means to nurture myself as the mother, such as pregnancy yoga and the illuminating information provided by birth gurus who knew about this state of being – though they may have called it by another name. If a woman cannot find the means to be nurtured, and is surrounded by fear or hostility, she will not easily surrender to this state unless she has retained an innate innocence that helped her link to the "ape brain" state – often found in much younger women – that Ina May Gaskin referred to in her communication to me before I went into labour.

The way that the pregnant brain makes the woman feel more forgetful and less capable of strategising puts her by default into a state that could be referred to as "present moment consciousness". Though never described as such in this context, this state, known as "mindfulness", has historically been sought by people seeking enlightenment and peace. Practices to facilitate this, such as meditation, have been described in ancient Hindu, Buddhist and Taoist teachings and, more recently, have also been adopted by psychologists. Mindfulness techniques are part of yoga, are beneficial in reducing anxiety and stress, can be used to induce calmness and are beginning to be assessed scientifically in pregnancy.[146] There is a new, growing field of mindfulness cognitive therapy, which is proposed as a non-pharmacological means of dealing with a range of problems such as anxiety, depression, stress, chronic pain, anger, certain types of cancer, psoriasis, eating disorders and addictions. However, all of these practices aim to encourage awareness of the present moment, which releases entanglement of the mind from its skittering between future and past-orientated thoughts. In pregnancy, hormones endow women with these tendencies without specific training, although a nurturing environment can facilitate the ability to surrender to it. Being in the present moment helps people deal with uncertainty, which is an antidote to the consequences of an anxious society that finds it difficult to negotiate the intellectual concept of risk. German sociologist Ulrich Beck, in his book *Risk Society*,[147] says that "Risk is a systematic way of dealing with hazards and insecurities, induced and introduced by modernisation itself. It infers that society is becoming more anxious and that the notion of risk is both a symptom and a cause of modern societal angst."

Obstetrics clearly has a crucial role to play when there are medical problems, but to view all pregnancies through the lens of risk-aversion medical culture does a disservice to those women who are capable of discovering the benefits of natural birth. Fear of childbirth really does prevent women from discovering their inner wisdom. Playwright Eve Ensler, author of *The Vagina Monologues*,[148] says in the context of society and risk,

> *I am proposing that we reconceive the dream. That we consider what would happen if security were not the point of our existence. That we find freedom, aliveness, and power not from what contains, locates, or protects us but from what dissolves, reveals, and expands us.*[149]

Those whose thinking is dominated by one side of the brain find it very difficult to appreciate the feelings of those dominated by the other side. A left-brain-dominated thinker finds it very difficult to appreciate what a right-brain-dominated thinker feels is important and visa versa. Hence my previous analogy of it being comparable to the notion of describing colours to a blind person. Hardened scientists may never be able to relate to or attain the consciousness of inner wisdom birthing because it is outside the parameters of the way they construct their reality or their mental processes, and years of discussion and study would bring them no nearer to it. Prior to my own pregnancy, certain aspects of birthing remained an intellectualisation for me until I experienced them first hand.

Despite some great discomforts and pain during my pregnancy, I derived a great deal of inner peace by accessing the right brain. When my consciousness rested in this place, my fear of labour dissolved of its own accord, priming my instinctual processes and improving my contractions. This softening of mind and body allowed an easier passage for my baby to enter the world.

During pregnancy, some women experience synaesthesia, a neurologically based phenomenon in which stimulation of one sensory or cognitive pathway leads to automatic, involuntary experiences in a second sensory or cognitive pathway. I myself found that communication with my baby took the form of seeing colours in my inner mind when I touched my belly. A labouring woman can feel and sense what her body and baby need to birth with inner vision of the organs and cells, especially if she has been coached into it with yoga. This is part of the dawning of inner wisdom.

The fewer analytic, worrisome or strategising thoughts a woman has, the more she is able to be open up the facility of instinctive maternal wisdom about the birth process.[150] Normal birth is instinctually programmed into women, but many have forgotten this. Birthing centres that allow women to get into this mental space but have a medical safety-net discretely available if necessary, are a good middle ground allowing women to have access to the best of both worlds. I don't believe that doctors will ever be the guardians of inner birthing wisdom – it is more the territory of midwives, doulas, yoga teachers and birthing gurus – but if they can acknowledge that there is another world of amazing life-enhancing birthing to be had, then they can get on with their jobs, dealing with medical problems whilst still being sensitive to and not dismissive of the greater gifts of the normal birth process. Doctors should also be aware that the chemical and hormonal state of pregnancy and normal birth has a wider impact than on the individual itself: societal behavioural issues are also at stake. Allowing the hormones that promote altruism and love to unfold in a natural way is a very important factor in this.

A week after I gave birth, I noticed my left-brain activity returning. I felt a sort of mourning for that pregnancy state of consciousness because I noticed that left-brain processes were accompanied by a background anxiety created by thinking once again about the past and the future. This is when I fully realised the beauty and wonder of that special opportunity of pregnancy consciousness. To access that state again, I knew I would have to practise meditation or live in the present moment with my baby as a kind of living meditation. This requires more intention or effort than being gifted inner birthing wisdom in pregnancy by Mother Nature.

CHAPTER 8
WOMEN, BIRTH AND SOCIETY

It wasn't until my own deeply personal experience of natural childbirth that I truly contextualised the correlation between the style of birth and the longer-term implications for the mother and child's contribution to society. As an obstetrician, there is no question of the importance of saving mothers' lives, hence my interest in safer motherhood issues, particularly in developing countries. I was interested in helping to reduce death or severe illness from excessive bleeding after childbirth and also in making labour as efficient as possible, which led to my research into Misoprostol, a drug that has a potential role in this area of medicalised birth. Using medicines to contain and control natural mayhem and inefficiency seemed to me a worthy, logical task to pursue. The intention behind conducting such research was to help women, and the method of investigation through randomised controlled trials looked at short-term but important outcomes concerning fixed episodes of pregnancy. Because of the logistics and levels of funding involved, clinical trials (research studies) rarely follow up their subjects over long periods of time, especially not the long-term psychological sequelae of medical interventions, as was the case with my research. At that time however, I was unaware that a mother's utilising of her own natural oxytocin bestowed upon her and her child emotional benefits. I, like many of my colleagues, was only aware of the mechanical implications of hormones and drugs that caused the womb to contract.

I have reflected many times throughout my life on a strong feeling of intuition I experienced when handling a case of catastrophic postpartum haemorrhage whilst training in obstetrics and doing my research on Misoprostol. It was a case in which a woman's womb failed to contract down efficiently after delivering the baby and placenta, and I remember vividly having to do internal and external massage on her womb throughout the night, taking turns with a consultant obstetrician. Eventually, by the morning, after several hours of massage, the woman's womb stayed contracted and her body started to repair itself. We were all thankful we had avoided the last resort of a hysterectomy to stop the bleeding. Nevertheless I still remember the strong feeling of intuition bubbling repetitively through my head, that the woman had a lack of love in her life, although I did not vocalise this. It is quite interesting for me to note that the endogenous oxytocin is now known colloquially as the "love" hormone; the importance of the presence or absence of this hormone during labour has been discussed earlier, but, during my training, I had not yet seen the full implications of a lack of love, emotional support and high levels of fear on the ability of a womb to contract. With regard to my research into Misoprostol, the look of horror on Ina May Gaskin's face when I discussed the subject with her spoke volumes. She prompted me to reflect on her opinion that although Misoprostol may be efficient at shortening labours, the rapidity of such labours made it far from a gentle birth, especially with the doses that were used in its early stages. This was not the only cause of her dismay on the subject: in the United States there had been instances of doctors misusing the drug for convenience, allowing them to practise "daylight obstetrics". This subject is well described on her website.[66] However, in Britain the use of this drug has been far more cautious than in the United States, for several reasons. One is that "daylight obstetrics" is more often seen in private practice, and because the majority of women in Britain have their babies in the government-provided NHS, it is not a widespread phenomenon in this country. Furthermore, in Britain there is greater organisational control than in the United States, through health policy and guidelines, to restrict induction of labour to women who need it for medical reasons only. I believe that the use of Misoprostol can be compared to internet usage: it can be a useful tool but it can also be abused. Further research has discovered much smaller doses to be both effective and gentler.

The understanding that normal birth can be a truly inspirational experience, rather than painful and traumatic, is not really covered in undergraduate or postgraduate medical education. The emotional benefits of normal labour do not motivate clinical research, which is more concerned with a mechanistic model of childbirth. Doctors act within the education they receive and to the best of their knowledge, mostly with noble motivation. When the cultural framework of science and medicine does not include knowledge of the benefits of "gentle" birth, then doctors almost unknowingly perpetuate the cycle of medicalised births. The idea of inspirational, transformative birth resonates so much with right-brain thought processes, that an individual who interprets life predominantly through logical left-brain analysis can find it impossible to comprehend why the concept is so important to women. I have met a few colleagues with this frame of mind, but with the aid of new government initiatives, such as encouraging patient-centred care, and edicts that ensure health professionals improve the quality of the patient's journey through the healthcare system, British healthcare is evolving. In my hospital, pregnant women are hugely enthusiastic about the availability of the maternity acupuncture service, which, although not a clinical priority for funding, is kept running because the hospital emphasises patient-centred care and choice.

Ina May was heartened to hear about the development of patient-centred care in British obstetrics. Women are extraordinarily sensitive in pregnancy – softened emotionally and physically. Being in a nurturing, supportive environment that respects their physical limits during this special time is paramount. Because of the potential shedding of emotional armour at this point, it can also provide a chance to re-invent one's emotional baseline. If there are any subconscious fears and anxieties, the inner-wisdom conscious that unfolds (if allowed) can really bring unexpected solutions to trapped loops of thought that inhibit the body from achieving its physiological best. Ina May's observations back this up. She has described occasions when labour has stopped progressing, but how, through her trusting relationship with the labouring woman, she was able to discover that a distressing psychological conundrum had surfaced within the woman. Such concerns were so private that they usually remained unvoiced unless there had been a trusting relationship. In some cases, Ina May was instrumental in helping to resolve the issue, and womb dilation then resumed progress. This kind of insight is impossible to detect in usual midwifery and obstetric practices because of the current system on a labour ward in which a midwife may have to look after several labouring women at the same time, with an obstetrician visiting as necessary, and perhaps called on suddenly to fix the problem with drugs or mechanistic solutions. Ina May's experience illustrates that artificial oxytocin or operative deliveries may not be the only solution for inefficient labours. We already know that continuous emotional support during labour is more powerful than any medical intervention in helping a woman to achieve a normal delivery.

At the same conference where I met Ina May, Joseph Chilton Pearce spoke about the prenatal neuro-developmental consequences of maternal stress throughout pregnancy. He eloquently described, through his synthesis of the Triune Brain Theory,[131] how babies born to mothers who experience prolonged severe psychological stress during their pregnancy can potentially have larger-than-average hind-brains and proportionately smaller fore-brains. The converse was true for babies born to mothers who felt nurtured and stress-free throughout their pregnancies. Joseph Chilton Pearce drew from the work of Paul MacLean,[131] an American physician and neuroscientist who made significant contributions in the fields of physiology, psychiatry and brain research through his work at Yale Medical School and the National Institute of Mental Health. MacLean proposed that through a process of evolution, the hind-brain (older in evolution) was broadly associated with neurological structures that contend with survival emotions such as "fight or flight" mechanisms or anger/hostility, whereas the fore-brain (newer in evolution), broadly, deals with more sociable emotional qualities. MacLean's research work suggested that, as it grew, the fetus re-enacted human neurological and emotional evolution so that the mother, during pregnancy, could potentiate types of fetal development. If the emotional state of the mother has the potential to produce lasting effects on the fetus, this has far-reaching implications for how we organise pregnancy care if we want to help produce babies with the optimum emotional neurodevelopmental hardwiring, where aggressive tendencies are minimised, and thereby contribute to a more peaceable society.

There is also a body of evidence[151-158] from independent prospective studies that if a mother is stressed while pregnant, her child is substantially more likely to have emotional or cognitive problems, including an increased risk of attention deficit/hyperactivity, anxiety and language delay. It seems that activity of the stress-responsive hypothalamic-pituitary-adrenal (HPA) axis and one of its hormonal end-product, cortisol, are involved in these effects on both mother and fetus. Elevated prenatal cortisol has been associated with several negative conditions including aborted fetuses, excessive fetal activity, delayed fetal growth and development, prematurity and low birth-weight, attention and temperament problems in infancy, externalizing problems in childhood, and psychopathology and chronic illness in adulthood. Because maternal prenatal cortisol crosses the placenta and influences other aspects of the prenatal environment, these effects on the fetus and its later development are not surprising. Cortisol is not the only body chemical to be affected by prenatal stress. Substances called pro-inflammatory cytokines IL-1B and IL-6 are stimulated by lymphocytes. White blood cells are also elevated, which suggests that stress during pregnancy affects the function of immune-system cells.[159] These findings further support the notion that prenatal stress alters maternal physiology and immune function in a manner consistent with increased risk of pregnancy complications such as pre-eclampsia and premature labour.

It is worth reiterating that if a woman has a stressful time during pregnancy due to uncontrollable circumstances, she shouldn't chastise herself for the potential impact this may have on her child's development; after all, humans have an enormous capacity to rise above all kinds of adversity and triumph. I myself had a stressful time during the first half of my pregnancy until I could actually start my birth preparation, but my subsequent interpretation of this, through inner communication with my baby, was that it was his way of re-directing me. Some fetuses are not necessarily passive victims of their mother's or society's folly, although others may be vulnerable.

Many commentators from different scientific and social disciplines look at birth in its broader context within society, rather than as a single, isolated event. Pre-and perinatal psychobiologists, child development experts, psycho-historians, life-course epidemiologists, anthropologists, ethologists, some obstetricians, birth activists and female rights activists have turned their attention to the potential impact of womb factors on the health of children and adults. We know from science that womb factors can programme into the fetus a predisposition to adult physical illnesses such as heart disease and hypertension.[160] However, there is growing evidence that the type of birth may have an effect on the emotional well-being of the baby and on into adulthood. Obstetrician Michel Odent keeps a database of such studies on his website[161] in an effort to bring some consilience to this area. Frederick LeBoyer says that difficulties encountered during childbirth can almost subconsciously affect our adult behaviour: [127]

The memory of birth and the terror that accompanies it
remains in each one of us.
But since it is so loaded with fear and pain, it
lies dormant and totally repressed, like a dreadful
secret at the bottom of our unconscious, like a
ship on the ocean floor.
But it is there, although we don't always know it.
Just like a name can be in our memory, but if it is
linked with unpleasant overtones, we think we can't
remember it.
Then again you might say if it is buried so deeply,
why dig it up, why not just let it rest?
Maybe we can't.
It is constantly trying to surface, and expresses itself
in our nightmares, our myths, our most
secret irrational inhibitions.
One could almost say that the root of all anguish
is an unconscious memory of birth and its
terrors.

We know that a traumatic birth is associated with birth asphyxia, mother and fetal injury and post-traumatic stress disorders. It is also associated with less mother and baby bonding, which has a subsequent impact on child-rearing and the child's emotions.[121;162-164] This might cause one to reach the seemingly logical conclusion that it is safer to avoid the birth process altogether, and opt for a caesarean section from the outset. In fact, a former colleague of mine, Raghad Al Mufti, published a much-quoted survey that would seem to support this idea. When obstetricians were asked what type of delivery they would select for themselves, the overwhelming response was planned elective caesarean section.[165] But caesarean section is linked with reduced mother-baby bonding and more medical risks compared to normal birth,[96;97] so it is not simply a question of offering caesarean section to all women to avoid the birth trauma.

There is evidence that the physiological process of labour has a particular role in developing nurturing emotional qualities in the mother and improving mother and baby bonding. A complex blend of hormones released during labour is vitally important in promoting nurturing qualities in the mother. Specifically, natural oxytocin, the hormone that doctors associate with producing womb contractions and the process of breastfeeding, has other important behavioural effects. When oxytocin is injected into virgin sheep, they develop maternal nurturing behaviour. Conversely, female rats given oxytocin antagonists after giving birth do not exhibit typical maternal behaviour.[166-168] Oxytocin has also been linked to being a mediator of emotional response during sexual intercourse and orgasm,[169] whilst in animals it has been implicated in promoting monogamy.[170] There are human social experiments that demonstrate the association between oxytocin and feelings of trust and generosity between people.[83;171] Oxytocin helps to make faces more familiar and aids the interpretation of facial expressions of emotion.[172-174] It is deficient in people with autism, and, as such, is being considered as a potential treatment to improve their ability to interact socially.[175-177] Women will experience the highest concentrations of oxytocin during normal labour just before birth,[178] so by actively avoiding labour through an elective caesarean section when there is no medical reason, a woman may indirectly deprive herself of this natural opportunity to let oxytocin influence the neurochemistry of nurturing, love, ecstasy and trust within her body. This may suggest it is better to have a non-emergency intrapartum caesarean section, although these are known to have more operative risks than an elective caesarean section. Perhaps this is a logical point at which to remember that most women have the innate ability to deliver normally and it is only the minority of women who have medical problems in pregnancy that require medical delivery.

Obstetrics or birthing can sometimes, in the minority of women, encounter unexpected life threatening emergencies, and to save lives, some trauma is experienced. But even for the majority of women who can have a normal birth, the concept of a gentle birth is quite alien in the current medical climate. I discovered during my own pregnancy and labour that with adequate birth preparation and accessing the inner-wisdom state, it was possible to experience a gentle birth. That is not to say that there was no pain because there was…but it only lasted a short time and "present moment" consciousness altered my perception of discomfort.

Birth preparation is not the only factor in helping the mother to experience a gentle birth. The right birthing environment is equally important. Oxytocin is thought to be a mediator of love and is influenced by fear,[82] therefore anxiety or fear can retard oxytocin manufacture and hence reduce womb contractions. It is clear that continuous emotional support and a homely, relaxed, non-clinical environment with a non-anxious midwife or doctor can increase a woman's state of trust and subsequent oxytocin excretion. A quiet, non-stimulatory environment that doesn't distract a woman away from her innate body wisdom also helps tremendously. Although it is necessary to monitor whether the labouring woman and baby stay healthy, clinical discretion should be exercised: each blood-pressure measurement is an intrusion into that state of misty, right-brain consciousness, free from strategising or anxiety, which lets a woman's body get on with the art of birthing. As Michel Odent says, we need to "rediscover basic needs of labouring women" to achieve normal birth because it has been forgotten at the present time.[20] Ina May Gaskin confirms this from a midwifery perspective:

> *Simply put, when there is no homebirth in a society, or when homebirth is driven completely underground, essential knowledge of women's capacities in birth is lost to the people of that society – to professional caregivers, as well as to the*

women of childbearing age themselves. The disappearance of knowledge once commonly held paves the way for over-medicalization of birth and the risks which this poses. Nothing in medical literature today communicates the idea that women's bodies are well designed for birth. [179]

Until my own pregnancy, I myself was deeply entrenched in that medical culture owing to my education, and therefore I quite understand the difficultly in thinking your way out of it. It was my own experience that revealed the art of normal birth to me.

There is an outcry from birth activists that the caesarean-section rate is too high and must be lowered. However, doing so may result in more difficult vaginal births as you are just treating the tip of the iceberg of the problem and not addressing the root of the issue. As Odent frequently discusses,[180] without the optimum environment for normal births, caesarean sections will continue to be necessary, which leads us back to the issue of re-discovering the best conditions for normal birth. This art of birthing is not currently in medical or midwifery maternity guidelines because there are fewer and fewer normal births within the modern maternity care setting.

A key component of rediscovering the art of birth may lie in firstly examining our nutritional advice. If, currently, we promote a balanced diet, rich with vitamins, which does not produce allergies or put the baby at risk of any infections, are there other aspects of diet that may help a woman to achieve normal birth? We may need to consider why babies in modern societies are getting bigger and hence more difficult to birth – is this a reflection of current dietary advice? The Royal College of Obstetricians only recently (in 2010) issued advice on weight management before, during and after pregnancy. We should explore whether diet can improve the state of the womb and pelvic soft tissues to achieve peak condition for the day of labour. (The analogy to this is getting a car serviced so that it is in prime condition for the day of a long journey, rather than setting off with an un-serviced car that may break down.) If so, can this advice be tailored for body types? There is a belief in Ayruveda and Chinese medicine that certain foods produce lots of mucus and "gum up" one's body, slowing down cellular processes or body functions, which is worse in those predisposed to mucus or easy weight gain. Gowri Motha's nutritional advice is derived from this principle. She advocates avoiding these types of foods, particularly when pregnant and in the last trimester, to allow the uterus to motor along more easily in labour, and the pelvic soft tissues to become more stretchable, [34] although more research is needed to explore these issues. In addition to diet, other ways of preparing the soft tissues for birth are pregnancy yoga and massaging the perineum with oils in the last few weeks of pregnancy (which now has some evidence base). [181;182]

A second component of antenatal care is to help women become more confident of their bodies' ability to birth, a confidence that has been eroded since the advent of medicalised birth. Antenatal classes that only provide factual information about the biological mechanism of labour and all the modes of pain relief and types of medical intervention may be a necessary part of birthing education, but, at present, such classes are not geared specifically to building body confidence and helping to address fears and maternal stress issues. This is where pregnancy yoga, active birth classes and hypnotherapy may come in very useful to the mother, [33;183-185] as they provide very nurturing environments for pregnant women. These activities acknowledge the softening process of pregnancy, unlike most work environments experienced by pregnant working women. With time, such classes help as possible gateways for mothers to access their own inner wisdom, something that cannot be attained simply by receiving information about choices or having a theoretical birth plan. At present, the scientific study of psycho-prophylaxis is in its rudimentary stages and interventions to teach women how to relax, in theory, during pregnancy, with manuals and a small amount of time devoted to practise, may well be too intellectual and not practical enough when compared to yoga or a pregnancy hypnosis course. [186] When the hormone oxytocin is released as part of the stress responses in a woman, it buffers the fight or flight response and encourages her to tend children and gather with other women. When she actually engages in this tending or befriending, studies suggest that more oxytocin is released, which further counters stress and produces a calming effect. This calming response does not occur in men because testosterone – which men produce in high levels when they are under stress – seems to reduce the effects of oxytocin, whereas oestrogen appears to enhance it.[50-52] Interestingly, from a completely different stream of international investigation, researchers have found that in Bangladesh transmission of essential healthcare information is more effective through informal women's groups than official educational programmes,[85] indicating that the power of women chatting has been hugely underestimated until now!

With respect to theoretical birth plans, I and other obstetric colleagues have noticed that there is almost certainly a correlation between length and complicatedness of a birth plan and that of birth complications. Having very fixed plans about birth and a complicated birth plan are symptoms of too much left-brain strategising activity, which is the antithesis of right-brain "inner wisdom birthing" consciousness. It is my feeling that "overly cerebral" women have a harder time achieving normal birth because they find it hard to get into the "no-brain, just-being" zone that is required to maximise the natural secretion of oxytocin.

As mentioned before, other complementary therapies may also help and could provide a drug-free avenue for respite from some of the uncomfortable symptoms of pregnancy, reduce fear and anxiety and help with labour. There is still very little scientific evidence regarding their benefits, with the exception of pregnancy yoga, acupuncture and hypnotherapy.[132] Currently, research funding in this area suffers from a Catch-22 situation in which scientific panels often reject applications for Complementary and Alternative Medicine (CAM) research due to lack of scientific basis, but lack of research funds prevents the scientific basis from being established. British medical charities spend only an estimated 0.08-0.31% of available funds on CAM research,[187;188] so if a woman today wishes to try such a therapy, it may be because she knows someone who has benefitted from it or because she puts her trust in an experienced practitioner, or it may be from a wish to explore the area with a view to "suck it and see". If she wants evidence, she will have to wait longer; the medical profession will never be able to fully endorse CAM in policy until the evidence is available.

The final component in helping labouring women achieve their physiological best is to create the optimum environment for labour. Ensuring the surroundings are homely and comforting, and providing equipment for women to be active and upright for as long as possible would help and is relatively simple to arrange in birthing institutions. However, in most countries at the present time, there are more complex issues to be addressed in the healthcare environment. One is the behaviour of midwives themselves. According to Michel Odent, the present system prevents midwives from simply being "motherly". Hospital midwives are enveloped in a risk-management, protocol-driven, drug and epidural-culture that makes it difficult to keep their intuitive midwifery skill intact. Some midwives manage to keep the balance but some do not; how do we help midwives to be non-anxious labour companions? Anxiety is contagious, and if it is just a habit of mind, rather than reserved for genuine emergencies, it can really sabotage a woman's labour.

We also need to consider how best to maintain a woman's privacy, how to protect her from the sensory stimuli of other emergencies on the labour ward and how to provide non-intrusive, safe health-monitoring so that her birthing wisdom is not disturbed. Most fundamental of all, perhaps, is to obtain the resources to ensure that there is continuous, emotional support. Perhaps this is all that is required: experienced doula Liliana Lammers has told me she believes that all the previously mentioned types of birth preparation are probably not that important if the right birthing environment is in place, with non-intrusive, continuous emotional support throughout labour. They only become more important when the right sort of environment is not possible or guaranteed.

It appears, in summary, that there is mounting evidence to support three recommendations by those most experienced in natural childbirth; that is, women labour well (because natural oxytocin release is enhanced) when some or either of the following conditions are available to a labouring woman:

- A non-threatening environment with low lighting and the silent support or presence of an experienced midwife who respects the woman's privacy and allows her to maintain her dignity.

- The company of empathic women.
- A loving, supportive, sensuous relationship with a non-anxious husband or partner. This is depicted eloquently in the educational documentary film, *Orgasmic Birth*.[189]
- Anxious, fearful partners, just like other anxious carers, may actually impede natural labour.

The Midwife's Tale,[94] an oral history of the profession, records the findings of one of the earliest public debates in Britain on maternal mortality, at Central Hall, Westminster, in 1928, in which it was recognised that the midwife more often secures physiological (normal) labour because she is prepared to wait. Doctors, on the other hand, are "an expensive social instrument", owing to their long training. It is difficult for the doctor to spare the time from his other patients to wait on nature, yet the securing of labour is an important basic principle in preventative medicine. Impatience with nature leads to tampering with the normal birth process. To want to train as a doctor, one must be fascinated by preventing and helping illness. So medics come to the birthing process from a specific point of view, one that is quite different from the motivation to become a midwife. Through the skewed sector of patients from which doctors gather their experience, they acquire a certain amount of emotional charge from the obstetric complications they have dealt with. Some of the complications are horrendous, but as practitioners of a type of emergency medicine, we develop coping mechanisms to deal with them, although each case will form an indelible mark upon our psyche. So, based on such experiences, many doctors will want to do everything possible to avoid such situations arising in other women. In order to re-educate doctors about the requirements for normal birth, it is probably reasonable to emphasise during their training that helping women to attain those basic requirements is part of preventative medicine. Medical students spend time with midwives during their training, which provides a helpful snapshot of this allied profession and fosters respect, but also provides students with the crucial experience of normal birth. However, more often than not, medical students are itching to get on with the essentials of birthing pathology or illness and they know that they did not choose to train as a midwife, so although they are tested on the basics of normal birth practices, they see this as a stepping-stone to the area they are most interested in.

We may be able to change the system if, somehow, we can inculcate into the education process the idea that letting midwives get on with the art of normal birth is an aspect of preventative health, and that a medical intervention during labour, unless absolutely necessary, can put women on a conveyor belt of more interventions. If the very sound scientific information about the effects of stress and anxiety on pregnant women, on bonding and parenting skills, child behaviour and society is absorbed into the medical curriculum, then 'nurturing the mother' can be integrated into doctors' education in terms that are readily understood, rather than as a nebulous concept. Those doctors that enjoy being involved in normal births can then put on their best midwifery hats on those occasions. There will always be a need for doctors to deal with ill health in pregnancy; there will always be some woman who, despite the best preparation in the world, will need medical assistance for childbirth. These women should not be disappointed with themselves, because illness happens: genes, environment, physical limitations or just bad luck play their part, just as in all aspects of life...but at least doctors are there to help.

Normal birth empowers women and results in better bonding between mother and baby, hence it has a knock-on effect of building confidence with child rearing. It enables that surge of natural oxytocin, which may contribute to our capacity to love. By having the opportunity to access innate inner-birthing wisdom, through 'present moment' consciousness, normal birth gives women a tool for life for dealing with the risk-averse, anxious, technologically driven society we live in. Normal birth gives us an appreciation and respect for Mother Nature.

In his book, *Childbirth without Fear: The Principles and Practice of Natural Child Birth*, obstetrician Grantley Dick Read wrote his valuable insights into normal childbirth in the 1940s,[190] and he, too, understood its importance to society. Today, there is scientific evidence from many academic disciplines to support his ideas that normal childbirth is advantageous to society at large. Life course epidemiology is already revealing that fetal programming in the uterine environment has far-reaching effects on adult health as well as on early childhood physical and psychological influences.[191;192] Psychohistorian Lloyd deMause attributes aggressive tendencies and war to the effect of the birth experience and its consequences on child rearing,[193] while emotional stress and depression during pregnancy have been linked to behavioural disorders in children.[155-158] There have also been numerous scientific papers on medicalised birth and its association with adolescent and adult self-destructive behaviours.[120;121;162;164] Professor Kerstin Uvnäs-Moberg and her team of co-researchers have shown that obstetric interventions such as epidural analgesia, synthetic oxytocin intravenous infusions and elective caesarean sections lower endogenous postpartum oxytocin levels. This is subsequently reflected in bonding behaviour and correlated with less calm behaviours in infants at one year of age. They have also demonstrated that early skin-to-skin exposure enhances bonding and increases oxytocin levels as well as calming and reducing anxiety in mother and baby. In fact, the oxytocin behavioural system is the opposite to the "fight or flight" response to stress. Professor Uvnäs-Moberg asserts that the human oxytocic behavioural system promotes positive emotions and that normal birth amplifies this system within us.[194-195] This validates the social neurobiological theory that oxytocin encourages social cohesion through the neurobiology of maternal and pair bonding, thus also, conversely, providing insights into the origins of human violence[196].

Eve Ensler, author of The *Vagina Monologues*[148] and charity worker, particularly in the field of violence against women, has given insightful interviews in which she states that, in her view, the key to ending violence in Africa is to end violence against women. Women who have been raped and violated cannot bring up their children in a compassionate and empowered way. If women are respected and cared for in society, the next generation will reflect these values, breaking at last the cycle of perpetual violence. In Democratic Republic of Congo (DCR), for example, endemic violence against women constantly sabotages any possibility of gentle future generations. Nurturing women results in nurtured children, which in turn means a nurtured society. In Lloyd deMause's book, *The Emotional Life of Nations*,[193] he suggests that the shaping of a nation's emotional identity is greatly influenced by the quality of its mothering.

The problem of violence against women in DCR is an extreme example of a culture that does not understand the wider impact of not nurturing mothers. However, in some developed countries, mothers are not allowed to mother to the best of their abilities because of employment conditions and not reducing hazards in the work place, or lack of sufficient maternity leave that, for example, curtails the possibility of breastfeeding for the six months recommended by the World Health Organisation.[197] This crucial period of bonding between mother and child, and its effects on the child's potential to contribute to society, has been acknowledged in a recent report commissioned by the UK's Children's Society. *The Good Childhood Report* of February 2009 argues that governments should provide more flexible employment options for parents to allow them to bring up children with love, which in turn will result in a society with more "heart".[198]

Embarking on a normal birth can be by default because there are no medical options available, but it is also requires that we trust in ourselves and in nature. In the current societal climate, a non-medicalised birth is at odds with a "risk-averse" or "health-and-safety" obsessed psyche. In a passage from her book, *Insecure at Last: Losing it in Our Security Obsessed World*,[149] Eve Ensler writes:

> *Is it possible to live surrendering to the reality of insecurity, embracing it, allowing it to open us and transform us and be our teacher? What would we need in order to stop panicking, clinging, consuming, and start opening, giving – becoming more ourselves the less secure we realize we actually are?*

As I discussed earlier, medicine and medical environments cater to notions of safety, protection from harm, and curing ills. But in shaping the medical infrastructure to avoid harm in the minority of women who experience problems, the birth experience of the healthy majority has been tampered with adversely. This is a philosophical conundrum that our "one-size-fits-all" prophylactic medical practices will have to acknowledge and debate. We have to understand that risk-reduction strategy can actually introduce harm through tangential avenues.

Technology is useful, but when it is overused and combined with fear of the unknown, it can make us all lose contact with our own health-related "wisdom within".

It cannot be emphasised enough that normal birth is the safest type of birth, which is borne out by an interesting paradox regarding the relative safety of homebirth versus hospital birth for low-risk women. Women who labour at home have fewer interventions and a higher normal birth rate than women who deliver in hospital, who have more medical interventions and a lower normal birth rate despite the availability of medical technology to increase safety. For the baby, safety levels may vary with the training levels of the midwife's newborn-resuscitation skills, but overall, the risks do seem to be very small. I suspect that in both developed and developing countries, home-grown humanistic interventions, which help us to nurture mothers and improve their own habitual endogenous oxytocin, will reduce fear and anxiety as well as optimising contractions, bonding and breastfeeding. They will probably outdo any technological advances to improve the normal birth rate.

However, some feminist thinkers find this model of childbirth and the role of the mother problematic. According to French feminist writer and philosopher Elizabeth Badinter, "Good motherhood imposes new duties that weigh heavily on those who do not keep them. It contravenes the model we have worked for [and] which makes equality of the sexes impossible and women's freedom irrelevant. It is a step backwards." She has also said that, "Thanks to a coalition of ecologists, breastfeeding advocates and behavioural specialists, young women are facing increasing pressure to be perfect mothers who adhere to strict guidelines for how to care for their babies."[199] But in my own experience as a doctor and career woman, who has reached the top of her profession but had a water birth at home, the personal growth I experienced through natural childbirth gave rise to a transcendent feeling of personal empowerment that neither my career nor any ideas about gender equality has ever really matched. The insight that I gained through the experience of pregnancy, and which was not incorporated into obstetric training, was that birth was not an intellectual or technical event, but a rite of passage that opens doors into other dimensions of inner wisdom, feminine power and influence upon future generations.

CONCLUSION

Throughout this book I have discussed the benefits of normal, natural birth for mother and child, starting from my own experience. I have discussed the ways in which this can be achieved, and how we can try to overturn the routine medicalisation of our risk-averse world. Ultimately, however, the way in which our children are born has a much wider impact than on that of the individual family concerned; it shapes the collective thinking of our society as a whole.

Although left-brain orientated societies achieve expansion of territories and technological progress, unless this can be tempered with right-brain consciousness, its spin-off is aggression; this absence of love can spell disaster for humanity and, ultimately, for the natural world. If we don't put some effort into reversing the increasing tide of medicalised birth, we may be in danger of drastically altering the emotional foundation of society. Teaching our children to appreciate nature is crucial for our future, as our planet has become so disturbed by our lack of respect for it. Pregnancy care and the way in which we are born needs to be embedded into a wider, life-course perspective of physical and emotional health in parents and their children. Safety in labour is important, but so too are the beneficial, biological, behavioural consequences that normal birth bestows upon society. These are love, compassion, nurturing, understanding, trust and co-operation. As our population expands, resources become limited, and we all have to learn to live in closer proximity to one another, we need to promote health practices that encourage social cohesion rather than fragmentation. This really is a very important primary health issue and a significant ecological issue. Mothers are a gateway to fostering love within humanity and wield enormous power on the individual as well as the collective. Mothers give people heart from our wombs.

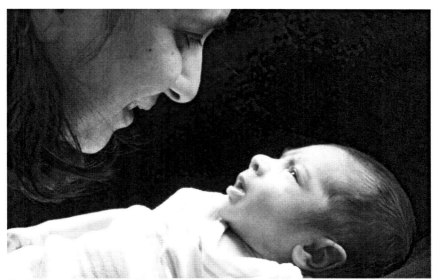

Sharing Love and Knowing.

EPILOGUE

The core of this book was written whilst I was breastfeeding my baby and still had a "pregnancy brain". The way a woman feels, thinks and prioritises when breastfeeding is very different from her state of mind when not pregnant. When breastfeeding is frequent prior to weaning, a woman acts far more from the heart than from the rational mind, with breastfeeding hormones exerting their behavioural effects. In fact, the nucleus of this book was written from the heart and I am glad that it was captured during that period. The scientific information was added after I stopped breastfeeding my baby at eleven months, so the book is a blend of my analytical mind with my new-found instinctual understanding of birth. Now that I have returned to clinical practice, my left-brain, logical thought-processes have returned and dominate my thinking. Ensconced once again in risk-oriented obstetrics and having witnessed some obstetric disasters, I sometimes look back and think, "Goodness me…did I really have a homebirth!" However, the whole experience that I have described in this book has left an indelible mark on me. Others have described inner-wisdom birthing in the past, but had I not experienced it for myself, I am not certain whether I could have logically accepted its existence. However, I can now confirm that it does exist. To access this state of being does not require belief or faith, it is just a gift of nature through the hormones of pregnancy, which happens when a woman surrenders to her femaleness. The state of inner wisdom that I have discussed has changed the way I deal with life because I have become more conscious of the present moment than ever before. The whole experience has boosted my right-brain activity, which helps a person become more comfortable with insecurity, and, as a result, I am far more trusting of nature and of natural processes. This is what I feel some women refer to when they describe natural birth as being empowering, quite apart from the enormous amount of self-respect that develops from it. A certain amount of strategising in professional life is necessary, but if this is also tempered with a more pragmatic approach, of taking life as it comes and having a receptive and flexible response to life's challenges, then it really helps one to negotiate life's chaos. Some of the most perfect solutions to life's problems are only visible in the moment and cannot be calculated.

APPENDIX

POLITICAL BIRTH MOVEMENTS

THE NATIONAL CHILDBIRTH TRUST

In 1944, Dr Grantley Dick-Reed wrote *Childbirth Without Fear*[190] following his observations of midwives with labouring women. He learned how midwives assisted labouring women to give birth without medication, using relaxation techniques. He also studied the fear-pain cycle and discovered that women who were not afraid of childbirth had less pain and fewer problems. His book inspired the founding of the National Childbirth Trust (NCT) in 1956 in Britain, which is a charity supporting parents-to-be. The NCT's original aims were:

- That women should be humanely treated during pregnancy and in labour; never hurried, bullied or ridiculed.
- That husbands should be present during labour if mutually desired.
- That analgesia should not be forced upon women in childbirth, nor should labour be induced merely to save time.
- That more emphasis should be given to self-regulated breastfeeding, that rooming-in should be allowed if the mother wants it and that future maternity units should be designed with this in mind.
- That a mother trained for natural childbirth should be allowed and encouraged to carry out her training fully during labour.

- That all mothers should be encouraged to use natural childbirth for the benefit of themselves and their babies, and that posters to this effect should be displayed at all antenatal clinics.
- That the idea fostered by many medical people today, that natural childbirth includes routine internal examination, routine administration of analgesia and routine episiotomy, should be dispelled.
- As childbirth is not a disease it should take place in the home wherever possible. If impossible, the maternity units should be homely and unfrightening, and in no way connected with hospital.

As an organisation, the NCT has, through its antenatal classes, been politically very instrumental in informing parents of the many choices available to them other than medicalised birth. The organisation also runs postnatal support groups and describes its aims thus:

> *A large majority of women in the UK give birth in hospital and action should be taken to increase their opportunities to give birth without unnecessary interventions. For many of those women with a more complex pregnancy requiring some medical care or ready access to emergency facilities, birth does not have to be a wholly medical event. It can be immensely rewarding for them to be actively involved in coping with contractions and pushing their baby into the world.* [200]

The NCT's sphere of influence has grown over the years, and the organisation now has representatives in key departments of health groups that determine health policy.

THE LAMAZE METHOD

This method was founded in 1951 when Dr Fernand Lamaze distilled his experiences from Russia into a coherent plan for improving the normal birth process for mothers. The method initially focused on the key components of childbirth education classes – relaxation, breathing techniques and continuous emotional support from the father and a specially trained nurse. It has evolved over many years from these original tenets, and its present philosophy is summarised below, by an organisation that is now known as Lamaze International, based in the United States:

- Birth is normal, natural and healthy.
- The experience of birth profoundly affects women and their families.
- Women's inner wisdom guides them through birth.
- Women's confidence and ability to give birth is either enhanced or diminished by the care provider and place of birth.
- Women have the right to give birth free from routine medical interventions.
- Birth can safely take place in homes, birth centres and hospitals.
- Childbirth education empowers women to make informed choices in healthcare, to assume responsibility for their health and to trust their inner wisdom.

SHEILA KITZINGER

Author, lecturer and birth activist, Sheila Kitzinger is a warrior against medicalised childbirth. She has a social anthropology background, focusing on birth and motherhood. She is particularly interested in women who are traumatised and unhappy after birth, and established the Birth Crisis Network as a helpline for women in Britain who have suffered a traumatic birth experience. She is also an activist concerned with the conditions of pregnant women and mothers in prison. An important part of her work is to provide as much information as possible about birthing options, so that women can make their own choices; the National Childbirth Trust has used her research to provide information to its members. She promotes the benefit of homebirth for low-risk women, and research areas include work on women's experiences of antenatal care, birth plans, induction of labour, epidurals, episiotomy, hospital care in childbirth, children's experiences of being present at birth, post-traumatic stress following childbirth and the many different messages that touch can give during childbirth.

Kitzinger has become an outspoken protester against the hegemony of technocratic birth, which in former years was the status quo. Her past efforts have catalysed change in maternity care, evidenced in the changes made in the NHS within the last five years through its National Service Frameworks, which has transformed the face of maternity care into a significantly more patient-orientated service.[64] For instance, induction of labour is now only recommended for clear medical indications and episiotomy is no longer performed routinely. Today, Kitzinger comments on obstetrics mainly through the eyes of traumatised women, such as in her book, *Birth Crisis*.[95] However, the domination of normal childbirth by the medical profession in Britain has significantly lessened in comparison to a few decades ago, and is further diminishing with policies such as Maternity Matters.[65] As such, hopefully, the massive frustration of natural-birth activists will abate.

ASSOCIATION FOR IMPROVEMENTS IN THE MATERNITY SERVICES (AIMS)

This is a British voluntary organisation that campaigns for improvements to childbirth services. The organisation's focus is to promote more normal births and it provides independent information about choices for pregnant women. It has specific campaigns focusing on the following: for women to be able to engage an independent midwife through the NHS when a homebirth midwife is not provided by the NHS; the right for women to choose the positions they prefer for labour and for giving birth; safe and adequate provision for homebirth by all NHS Trusts; reductions in the routine use of labour interventions, such as induction and electronic fetal monitoring; an end to routine ultrasound examination – the safety and efficacy of which have not been properly evaluated; reduction in the over-use of drugs in labour; reduction in caesarean operation rates to less than 10%; public right of access to maternity unit statistical data; and more evaluation before the widespread introduction of technologies and interventions.

SUZANNE ARMS

Suzanne Arms is based in the United States and is a well-known natural-birth activist, author, film- maker and public speaker and founder of the organisation Birthing the Future. Her focus is on holistic birth and the mother-baby bond, and her philosophy blends spirituality, feminism, ecology and mind-body science. Arms speaks from the perspective that the birth process has been damaged and dehumanised by technological medicine, and is an advocate for other women who have experienced emotional and physical birth trauma. She supports nurturing mothers and believes that the basis of love, peace, fear and violence stem from conditions in the womb.

FREE-BIRTHING

The desire for unassisted childbirth is a minority movement, but growing. The practice is not condoned by medical or midwifery professionals because of the lack of help available should a life-threatening complication arise. However, women attracted to this type of birthing experience give many reasons, including a dissatisfaction with medicalised birth. Other reasons include the belief that:

- Most interventions commonly used by the medical profession during a normal birth cause more harm than good.
- Birth is a normal function of the human body, not an illness.
- The mother will be more apt to follow the natural flow of her individual birth in an undisturbed birth setting, thus enabling her to find the optimum positions or techniques to birth her child safely.
- Birth is an intimate, sexual, and potentially orgasmic experience, and privacy is absolutely essential for any erotic aspect of birth.

Most free-birthers are keen practitioners of informed choice and self-care and want to take responsibility for their own health. However, some women who are planning an unassisted birth choose to have professional prenatal care as part of their birth preparation, to allow them to gauge their risk factors. Free-birthers also believe that choosing unassisted childbirth following proper nutrition, hygiene, prenatal self-care and psychological preparation is quite a different entity to unassisted childbirth because of poverty, ignorance, poor nutrition, poor hygiene and lack of empowerment, as found in the developing world.

REFERENCES

(1)   Appropriate technology for birth. Lancet 1985; 2(8452):436-437.

(2)   Hennekens CH, Buring JE. Epidemiology in Medicine. Boston, MA:
        Little, Brown; 1987.

(3)   Floyd R. Birth as an American Rite of Passage. 2nd ed. Berkeley, CA:
        University of California Press; 2003.

(4)   Turner VW. Betwixt and between: the liminal period in rites of
        passage, in Lessa WA, Vogt EZ, editors. Reader in Comparative
        Religion, an Anthropological Approach. 4th ed. New York, NY: Harper
        & Row; 1979.

(5)   Flower A, Liu JP, Chen S, Lewith G, Little P. Chinese herbal medicine
        for endometriosis. Cochrane Database Syst Rev 2009;(3):CD006568.

(6)   Jia LN, Wang XJ. [Clinical observation on treatment of 43 women with
        polycystic ovary syndrome based on syndrome differentiation]. Zhong
        Xi Yi Jie He Xue Bao 2006; 4(6):585-588.

(7)   Lian F. TCM treatment of luteal phase defect--an analysis of 60 cases.
        J Tradit Chin Med 1991; 11(2):115-120.

(8)   Tempest HG, Homa ST, Zhai XP, Griffin DK. Significant reduction of sperm disomy in six men: effect of traditional Chinese medicine? Asian J Androl 2005; 7(4):419-425

.(9)   You JS, Hu SY, Xiang QH, Li XL, Chen CH, Wang YH. [Effects of di-zhen granules on catecholamine transmitter and gonadotropin of clamacteric rats with deficiency of yin brings about the interior heat-syndrome]. Hunan Yi Ke Da Xue Xue Bao 2001; 26(1):33-36.

(10)   Zhang J, Li T, Zhou L, Tang L, Xu L, Wu T et al. Chinese herbal medicine for subfertile women with polycystic ovarian syndrome. Cochrane Database Syst Rev 2010;(9):CD007535.

(11)   Tempest HG, Homa ST, Zhai XP, Griffin DK. Significant reduction of sperm disomy in six men: effect of traditional Chinese medicine? Asian J Androl 2005; 7(4):419-425.

(12)   Luke B, Brown MB. Elevated risks of pregnancy complications and adverse outcomes with increasing maternal age. Hum Reprod 2007; 22(5):1264-1272.

(13)   Irwin MR. Human psychoneuroimmunology: 20 years of discovery. Brain Behav Immun 2008; 22(2):129-139.

(14)   Sylvia C. A Change of Heart: A Memoir. New York, NY: Grand Central Publishing; 1998.

(15)   Ball P. Cellular memory hints at the origins of intelligence. Nature 2008; 451(7177):385.

(16)   Helmreich RJ, Shiao SY, Dune LS. Meta-analysis of acustimulation effects on nausea and vomiting in pregnant women. Explore (NY) 2006; 2(5):412-421.

(17)   de Oliveira LF, Camboim C, Diehl F, Consiglio AR, Quillfeldt JA. Glucocorticoid-mediated effects of systemic oxytocin upon memory retrieval. Neurobiol Learn Mem 2007; 87(1):67-71.

(18)   Heinrichs M, Meinlschmidt G, Wippich W, Ehlert U, Hellhammer DH.
         Selective amnesic effects of oxytocin on human memory. Physiol
         Behav 2004; 83(1):31-38.

(19)   Lewis G. Confidential Enquiries into Maternal Deaths in the United
         Kingdom, Confidential Enquiry into Maternal and Child Health,
         CEMACH. Saving mothers' lives reviewing maternal deaths to make
         motherhood safer - 2003-2005 : the seventh report of the Confidential
         Enquiries into Maternal Deaths in the United Kingdom. London:
         CEMACH; 2007.

(20)   Odent M. New reasons and new ways to study birth physiology. Int J
         Gynaecol Obstet 2001; 75 Suppl 1:S39-S45.

(21)   Kisilevsky BS, Hains SM, Lee K, Xie X, Huang H, Ye HH et al. Effects
         of experience on fetal voice recognition. Psychol Sci 2003; 14(3):220-
         224.

(22)   Kisilevsky BS, Hains SM, Brown CA, Lee CT, Cowperthwaite B,
         Stutzman SS et al. Fetal sensitivity to properties of maternal speech
         and language. Infant Behav Dev 2009; 32(1):59-71.

(23)   Armour JA, Ardell JL. Neurocardiology. New York, NY: Oxford
         University Press; 1994.

(24)   Childre DL, Martin H. The HeartMath Solution: The Institute of
         HeartMath's Revolutionary Program for Engaging the Power of the
         Heart's Intelligence. New York, NY: HarperOne; 2009.

(25)   Marinelli R, Fuerst B, van der Zee H, McGinn A, Marinelli W. The heart
         is not a pump. A refutation of the pressure propulsion premise of heart
         function. Frontier Perspectives 1995; 5(1).

(26)   Raloff J. EMFs' Biological Influences: Electromagnetic fields exert
         effects on and through hormones. Science News 1998; 153(2):29-31.

(27)   Jankowski M, Danalache B, Wang D, Bhat P, Hajjar F, Marcinkiewicz
         M et al. Oxytocin in cardiac ontogeny. Proc Natl Acad Sci U S A 2004;
         101(35):13074-13079.

(28)   Paquin J, Danalache BA, Jankowski M, McCann SM, Gutkowska
         J. Oxytocin induces differentiation of P19 embryonic stem cells to
         cardiomyocytes. Proc Natl Acad Sci U S A 2002; 99(14):9550-9555.

(29)   Cherry N. Schumann Resonance and Sunspot Relations to Human
         Health Effects in Thailand. Natural Hazards 2003;(29):1.

(30)   Cohen M, Wohlers A. Is there a relationship between sunspot
         numbers and psychiatric admissions? Bioelectromagnetism,
         1998. Proceedings of the 2nd International Conference on
         Bioelectromagnetism. 15-18 February 1998. Melbourne Australia.
         [149-150]

(31)   Bellieni CV, Acampa M, Maffei M, Maffei S, Perrone S, Pinto I et al.
         Electromagnetic fields produced by incubators influence heart rate
         variability in newborns. Archives of Disease in Childhood Fetal and
         Neonatal Edition 2008; 93(4):F298-F301.

(32)   Dinsmore-Tuli U. Mother's Breath: A definitive guide to yoga breathing,
         sound and awareness practices for pregnancy, birth, post-natal
         recovery and mothering. London: Sitaram and Sons; 2006.

(33)   Balaskas J. Active Birth: The New Approach to Giving Birth Naturally.
         Boston, MA: Harvard Common Press; 1994.

(34)   Motha G, MacLeod KS. The Gentle Birth Method: The Month-by-
         Month Jeyarani Way Programme. London: Thorsons; 2004.

(35)   Chang SL, Lin KJ, Lin RT, Hung PH, Lin JG, Cheng JT. Enhanced
         insulin sensitivity using electroacupuncture on bilateral Zusanli
         acupoints (ST 36) in rats. Life Sciences 2006; 79(10):967-971.

(36)   Active Birth Centre. http://www.activebirthcentre.com. Accessed
         2009. Ref Type: Internet Communication

(37)   Sack O. www.oliversacks.com. Accessed 2009.
         Ref Type: Internet Communication.

(38)   Odent M. The Scientification of Love. London: Free Association
         Books; 1999.

(39)   Lokugamage AU, Refaey HE, Rodeck CH. Misoprostol and
         pregnancy: ever-increasing indications of effective usage. Curr Opin
         Obstet Gynecol 2003; 15(6):513-518.

(40)   Lokugamage AU, Forsyth SF, Sullivan KR, El RH, Rodeck CH.
         Randomized trial in multiparous patients: investigating a single vs.
         two-dose regimen of intravaginal misoprostol for induction of labor.
         Acta Obstet Gynecol Scand 2003; 82(2):138-142.

(41)   Lokugamage AU, Forsyth SF, Sullivan KR, El RH, Rodeck CH.
         Dinoprostone versus misoprostol: a randomized study of nulliparous
         women undergoing induction of labor. Acta Obstet Gynecol Scand
         2003; 82(2):133-137.

(42)   O'Brien P, Lokugamage AU, Guillebaud J, Rodeck CH. Use of
         misoprostol in third stage of labour. Lancet 2002; 359(9307):708-710.

(43)   Lokugamage AU, Paine M, Bassaw-Balroop K, Sullivan KR, Refaey
         HE, Rodeck CH. Active management of the third stage at caesarean
         section: a randomised controlled trial of misoprostol versus
         syntocinon. Aust N Z J Obstet Gynaecol 2001; 41(4):411-414.

(44)   Lokugamage AU, Sullivan KR, Niculescu I, Tigere P, Onyangunga F,
         El RH et al. A randomized study comparing rectally administered
         misoprostol versus Syntometrine combined with an oxytocin infusion
         for the cessation of primary post partum hemorrhage. Acta Obstet
         Gynecol Scand 2001; 80(9):835-839.

(45)   National Collaborating Centre for Women's and Children's Health
         (Great Britain), National Institute for Health and Clinical Excellence
         (Great Britain). Antenatal care: Routine care for the healthy pregnant
         woman. 2nd ed. London: RCOG Press; 2008.

(46)   Geissbuehler V, Stein S, Eberhard J. Waterbirths compared with
         landbirths: an observational study of nine years. Journal of Perinatal
         Medicine 2004; 32Berlin(4):308-314.

(47)   Birthing Matters. http://www.birthingmatters.co.uk. Accessed 2011.
         Ref Type: Internet Communication

(48)   Beckmann MM, Garrett AJ. Antenatal perineal massage for reducing
         perineal trauma. Cochrane Database Syst Rev 2006;(1):CD005123.

(49)   Jenkins MW. Pritchard MH. Hypnosis: practical applications and
         theoretical considerations in normal labour. Br J Obstet Gynaecol
         1993; 100(3):221-226.

(50)   Geary DC, Flinn MV. Sex differences in behavioral and hormonal
         response to social threat: commentary on Taylor et al. (2000). Psychol
         Rev 2002; 109(4):745-750.

(51)   Klein LC, Corwin EJ. Seeing the unexpected: how sex differences
         in stress responses may provide a new perspective on the
         manifestation of psychiatric disorders. Curr Psychiatry Rep 2002;
         4(6):441-448.

(52)   Taylor SE, Klein LC, Lewis BP, Gruenewald TL, Gurung RA, Updegraff
         JA. Biobehavioral responses to stress in females: tend-and-befriend,
         not fight-or-flight. Psychol Rev 2000; 107(3):411-429.

(53)   Campbell J. The Power of Myth. 1st ed. New York, NY: Doubleday;
         1988.

(54)   Jung CG, Hull RFC. The Archetypes and the Collective Unconscious.
         2nd ed ed. Princeton, NJ: Princeton University Press; 1980.

(55)   Ogden J, Shaw A, Zander L. Part 1. Womens' memories of homebirth 3-5 years on. British Journal of Midwifery 1997; 5(4):208-211.

(56)   Ogden J, Shaw A, Zander L. Part 2. Deciding on a homebirth: help and hindrance. British Journal of Midwifery 1997; 5(4):212-215.

(57)   Ogden J, Shaw A, Zander L. Part 3. A decision with a lasting effect. British Journal of Midwifery 1997; 5(4):216-218.

(58)   Ogden J, Shaw A, Zander L. Women's experience of having a hospital birth. British Journal of Midwifery 1998; 6(5):339-345.

(59)   Soderquist J, Wijma B, Wijma K. The longitudinal course of post-traumatic stress after childbirth. J Psychosom Obstet Gynaecol 2006; 27(2):113-119.

(60)   Zaers S, Waschke M, Ehlert U. Depressive symptoms and symptoms of post-traumatic stress disorder in women after childbirth. J Psychosom Obstet Gynaecol 2008; 29(1):61-71.

(61)   Jung CG, Read HE, Fordham M, Adler G, Hull RFC, Baynes HG. The Collected Works of C.G. Jung. London: Routledge and K. Paul; 1971.

(62)   Hodnett ED, Gates S, Hofmeyr GJ, Sakala C. Continuous Support for Women During Childbirth. Cochrane Database of Systematic Reviews 2007;(Issue 2. Art. No.: CD003766. DOI: 10.1002/14651858. CD003766.pub2).

(63)   Hatem M, Sandall J, Devane D, Soltani H, Gates S. Midwife-led versus other models of care for childbearing women. Cochrane Database Syst Rev 2008;(4):CD004667.

(64)   Department of Health DfEaS. National service framework for children, young people and maternity services: Executive summary. 40496. 14-9-2004. Crown. Ref Type: Report

(65)   Department of Health. Maternity matters: choice, access and
         continuity of care in a safe service. 3-4-2007. Crown. Ref Type: Report

(66)   Ina May Gaskin. http://www.inamay.com. Accessed 2009.
         Ref Type: Internet Communication

67)   Teijilingen ERV, Lowis G, McCafery P, Porter M. Midwifery and the
         Medicalisation of Childbirth. Nova Publishers; 2004.

(68)   Van der Mark EA, Spinhuis H. Successful Home Birth and Midwifery:
         The Dutch Model. Westport, CT: Bergin & Garvey; 1993.

(69)   de Jonge A, van der Goes BY, Ravelli ACJ, Amelink-Verburg MP, Mol
         BW, Nijhuis JG et al. Perinatal mortality and morbidity in a nationwide
         cohort of 529 688 low-risk planned home and hospital births.
         BJOG: An International Journal of Obstetrics & Gynaecology 2009;
         116(9):1177-1184.

(70)   Wax JR, Lucas FL, Lamont M, Pinette MG, Cartin A, Blackstone J.
         Maternal and newborn outcomes in planned home birth vs planned
         hospital births: a metaanalysis. Am J Obstet Gynecol 2010.

(71)   Ackermann-Liebrich U, Voegeli T, Gunter-Witt K, Kunz I, Zullig
         M, Schindler C et al. Home versus hospital deliveries: follow up study
         of matched pairs for procedures and outcome. Zurich Study Team.
         BMJ 1996; 313(7068):1313-1318.

(72)   Chamberlain G, Wraight A, Crowley P. Home births:
         the report of the 1994 confidential enquiry by the National Birthday
         Trust Fund. New York, NY: Parthenon Publishing Group; 1997.

(73)   Janssen PA, Saxell L, Page LA, Klein MC, Liston RM, Lee SK.
         Outcomes of planned home birth with registered midwife versus
         planned hospital birth with midwife or physician. CMAJ 2009; 181(6-
         7):377-383.

(74)   Johnson KC, Daviss BA. Outcomes of planned home births with
         certified professional midwives: large prospective study in North
         America. BMJ 2005; 330(7505):1416.

(75)   Woodcock HC, Read AW, Bower C, Stanley FJ, Moore DJ. A matched
         cohort study of planned home and hospital births in Western Australia
         1981-1987. Midwifery 1994; 10(3):125-135.

(76)   Koblinsky M, Timyan J, Gay J, Griffiths M, Kurz KM. The Health of
         Women: A Global Perspective. Boulder CO: Westview Press; 1993.

(77)   African Birth Collective. http://www.africanbirthcollective.org/.
         Accessed 2009. Ref Type: Internet Communication

(78)   Birth & Midwifery in Nepal. http://www.midwiferytoday.com/
         international/Nepal.asp. Accessed 2009. Ref Type: Internet
         Communication

(79)   Sakala C, Corry MP. Evidence-based maternity care: What it is and
         what it can achieve. 2008. New YorkChildbirth Connection, the
         Reforming States Group and the Milbank Memorial Fund.
         Ref Type: Report

(80)   Kennell J, Klaus M, McGrath S, Robertson S, Hinkley C. Continuous
         emotional support during labor in a US hospital. A randomized
         controlled trial. JAMA 1991; 265(17):2197-2201.

(81)   Baumgartner T, Heinrichs M, Vonlanthen A, Fischbacher U, Fehr E.
         Oxytocin shapes the neural circuitry of trust and trust adaptation in
         humans. Neuron 2008; 58(4):639-650.

(82)   Debiec J. Peptides of love and fear: vasopressin and oxytocin
         modulate the integration of information in the amygdala. Bioessays
         2005; 27(9):869-873.

(83)   Zak PJ, Stanton AA, Ahmadi S. Oxytocin increases generosity in
         humans. PLoS One 2007; 2(11):e1128.

(84)   Zeki S. The neurobiology of love. FEBS Lett 2007; 581(14):2575-2579.

(85)   Azad K, Barnett S, Banerjee B, Shaha S, Khan K, Rego AR et
         al. Effect of scaling up women's groups on birth outcomes in three
         rural districts in Bangladesh: a cluster-randomised controlled trial.
         Lancet 2010; 375(9721):1193-1202.

(86)   Kleinman A, Sung LH. Why do indigenous practitioners successfully
         heal? Soc Sci Med Med Anthropol 1979; 13 B(1):7-26.

(87)   Cassidy T. Birth: the surprising history of how we are born. 1st ed ed.
         New York, NY: Atlantic Monthly Press; 2006.

(88)   Seneviratne HR. The caesarean section rate is rising. Attempts to curb
         it must be based on good obstetric care. http://www.cmj.slma.lk/
         cmj4604/119.htm. Accessed 2010.

(89)   Anderson GM. Making sense of rising caesarean section rates. BMJ
         2004; 329(7468):696-697.

(90)   Hsu KH, Liao PJ, Hwang CJ. Factors affecting Taiwanese women's
         choice of Cesarean section. Soc Sci Med 2008; 66(1):201-209.

(91)   Fitzpatrick L. The Labor Market. Time. 20-3-2008.
         Ref Type: Magazine Article

(92)   Royal College of Obstetricians and Gynaecologists (Great Britain),
         Clinical Effectiveness SU, Royal College of Midwives (Great Britain),
         Royal College of Anaesthetists (Great Britain), National Childbirth
         Trust (Great Britain). The national sentinel caesarean section audit
         report. London: RCOG; 2001.

(93)   Nuland SB. The Doctors' Plague: Germs, Childbed Fever and the
         Strange Story of Ignac Semmelweis (Great Discoveries). London: W.
         W. Norton & Co; 2004.

(94) Leap N, Hunter B. The Midwife's Tale: An Oral History from Handywoman to Professional Midwife. London: Scarlet Press; 1993.

(95) Kitzinger S. Birth crisis. London: Routledge; 2006.

(96) Forster DA, McLachlan HL. Breastfeeding initiation and birth setting practices: a review of the literature. J Midwifery Women's Health 2007; 52(3):273-280.

(97) Smith LJ. Impact of birthing practices on the breastfeeding dyad. J Midwifery Women's Health 2007; 52(6):621-630.

(98) Enkin M. A Guide to Effective Care in Pregnancy and Childbirth. 3rd ed ed. Oxford: Oxford University Press; 2000.

(99) Alfirevic Z, Devane D, Gyte GML. Continuous cardiotocography (CTG) as a form of electronic fetal monitoring (EFM) for fetal assessment during labour. Cochrane Database of Systematic Reviews 2006;(Issue 3. Art. No.: CD006066. DOI: 10.1002/14651858.

(100) Rusconi F, Galassi C, Forastiere F, Bellasio M, De SM, Ciccone G et al. Maternal complications and procedures in pregnancy and at birth and wheezing phenotypes in children. Am J Respir Crit Care Med 2007; 175(1):16-21.

(101) Bedford Russell AR, Murch SH. Could peripartum antibiotics have delayed health consequences for the infant? BJOG 2006; 113(7):758-765.

(102) Glasgow TS, Young PC, Wallin J, Kwok C, Stoddard G, Firth S et al. Association of intrapartum antibiotic exposure and late-onset serious bacterial infections in infants. Pediatrics 2005; 116(3):696-702.

(103) Gronlund MM, Lehtonen OP, Eerola E, Kero P. Fecal microflora in healthy infants born by different methods of delivery: permanent changes in intestinal flora after cesarean delivery. J Pediatr Gastroenterol Nutr 1999; 28(1):19-25.

(104)   Penders J, Thijs C, Vink C, Stelma FF, Snijders B, Kummeling I et al.
         Factors influencing the composition of the intestinal microbiota in early
         infancy. Pediatrics 2006; 118(2):511-521.

(105)   Molloy EJ, O'Neill AJ, Grantham JJ, Sheridan-Pereira M, Fitzpatrick
         JM, Webb DW et al. Labor promotes neonatal neutrophil survival and
         lipopolysaccharide responsiveness. Pediatr Res 2004; 56(1):99-103.

(106)   Almeida EC, Nogueira AA, Candido dos Reis FJ, Rosa e Silva JC.
         Cesarean section as a cause of chronic pelvic pain. Int J Gynaecol
         Obstet 2002; 79(2):101-104.

(107)   Getahun D, Oyelese Y, Salihu HM, Ananth CV. Previous cesarean
         delivery and risks of placenta previa and placental abruption. Obstet
         Gynecol 2006; 107(4):771-778.

(108)   Lyell DJ, Caughey AB, Hu E, Daniels K. Peritoneal closure at primary
         cesarean delivery and adhesions. Obstet Gynecol 2005; 106(2):275-
         280.

(109)   Morales KJ, Gordon MC, Bates GW, Jr. Postcesarean delivery
         adhesions associated with delayed delivery of infant. Am J Obstet
         Gynecol 2007; 196(5):461-466.

(110)   Nisenblat V, Barak S, Griness OB, Degani S, Ohel G, Gonen R.
         Maternal complications associated with multiple cesarean deliveries.
         Obstet Gynecol 2006; 108(1):21-26.

(111)   Taylor LK, Simpson JM, Roberts CL, Olive EC, Henderson-Smart DJ.
         Risk of complications in a second pregnancy following caesarean
         section in the first pregnancy: a population-based study. Med J Aust
         2005; 183(10):515-519.

112)   Kennare R, Tucker G, Heard A, Chan A. Risks of adverse outcomes
         in the next birth after a first cesarean delivery. Obstet Gynecol 2007;
         109(2 Pt 1):270-276.

(113)   Tita AT, Landon MB, Spong CY, Lai Y, Leveno KJ, Varner MW et al.
         Timing of elective repeat cesarean delivery at term and neonatal
         outcomes. N Engl J Med 2009; 360(2):111-120.

(114)   Ransjo-Arvidson AB, Matthiesen AS, Lilja G, Nissen E, Widstrom AM,
         Uvnas-Moberg K. Maternal analgesia during labor disturbs newborn
         behavior: effects on breastfeeding, temperature, and crying. Birth
         2001; 28(1):5-12.

(115)   Moore ER, Anderson GC, Bergman N. Early skin-to-skin contact for
         mothers and their healthy newborn infants. Cochrane Database Syst
         Rev 2007;(3):CD003519.

(116)   IBFAN Proposal for a common action, Breastfeeding – the best
         start for a healthy life. High Level Group meeting of Member states
         and the European Commission; 2006.

(117)   Students of Central Saint Martin's College of Art & Design. Get Britain
         Breast Feeding Poster Campaign. 2008. Best Beginnings.
         Ref Type: Art Work

(118)   WHO Forum on the Marketing of Food and Non-alcoholic Beverages
         to Children. Marketing of Food and Non-alcoholic Beverages to
         Children. 2-5-2006. World Health Organisation.
         Ref Type: Report

(119)   Nyberg K, Buka SL, Lipsitt LP. Perinatal medication as a potential risk
         factor for adult drug abuse in a North American cohort. Epidemiology
         2000; 11(6):715-716.

(120)   Jacobson B, Nyberg K, Gronbladh L, Eklund G, Bygdeman M,
         Rydberg U. Opiate addiction in adult offspring through possible
         imprinting after obstetric treatment. BMJ 1990; 301(6760):1067-1070.

(121)   Jacobson B, Bygdeman M. Obstetric care and proneness of offspring
         to suicide as adults: case-control study. BMJ 1998; 317(7169):1346-
         1349.

(122)   Birthworks International. http://www.birthworks.org/primalhealth.
         Accessed 2010.
         Ref Type: Internet Communication

(123)   Gaskin IM. Spiritual Midwifery. 4th ed ed. Summertown, TN: Book Pub.
         Co; 2002.

(124)   Gaskin IM. Home Birth—Why It's Necessary . 14-1-2007. Ina May
         Gaskin Productions.
         Ref Type: Internet Communication

(125)   Bruner JP, Drummond SB, Meenan AL, Gaskin IM. All-fours maneuver
         for reducing shoulder dystocia during labor. J Reprod Med 1998;
         43(5):439-443.

(126)   Gaskin IM. Maternal Death in the United States: A Problem Solved or
         a Problem Ignored? J Perinat Educ 2008; 17(2):9-13.

(127)   Leboyer F. Birth Without Violence: New Edition. Rochester,
         VT: Inner Traditions – Bear & Company; Rev Ed edition, 2002.

(128)   Leboyer F. Loving Hands: The Traditional Art of Baby Massage. New
         York, NY: Newmarket Press; 1997.

(129)   Procianoy RS, Mendes EW, Silveira RC. Massage therapy improves
         neurodevelopment outcome at two years corrected age for very low
         birth weight infants. Early Hum Dev 2009.

(130)   Mercogliano C, Debus K. An Interview with Joseph Chilton Pearce.
         Journal of Family Life 5[1]. 1999.
         Ref Type: Magazine Article

(131)   MacLean PD. The Triune Brain in Evolution Role in Paleocerebral
         Functions. New York, NY: Plenum Press; 1990.

(132)   Smith CA, Collins CT, Cyna AM, Crowther CA. Complementary and
         alternative therapies for pain management in labour. Cochrane
         Database Syst Rev 2006;(4):CD003521.

(133)   Frey UH, Scharmann P, Lohlein C, Peters J. P6 acustimulation
         effectively decreases postoperative nausea and vomiting in high-risk
         patients. Br J Anaesth 2009; 102(5):620-625.

(134)   Jewell D, Young G. Interventions for nausea and vomiting in early
         pregnancy. Cochrane Database Syst Rev 2003;(4):CD000145.

(135)   Vermani E, Mittal R, Weeks A. Pelvic girdle pain and low back pain in
         pregnancy: A Review. Pain Pract 2009.

(136)   Holst L, Wright D, Haavik S, Nordeng H. Safety and efficacy of herbal
         remedies in obstetrics-review and clinical implications. Midwifery
         2009.

(137)   Dugoua JJ, Perri D, Seely D, Mills E, Koren G. Safety and efficacy
         of blue cohosh (Caulophyllum thalictroides) during pregnancy and
         lactation. Can J Clin Pharmacol 2008; 15(1):e66-e73.

(138)   Beckmann MM, Garrett AJ. Antenatal perineal massage for reducing
         perineal trauma. Cochrane Database Syst Rev 2006;(1):CD005123.

(139)   Furlan AD, Imamura M, Dryden T, Irvin E. Massage for low-back pain.
         Cochrane Database Syst Rev 2008;(4):CD001929.

(140)   Moyer CA, Rounds J, Hannum JW. A meta-analysis of massage
         therapy research. Psychol Bull 2004; 130(1):3-18.

(141)   Procianoy RS, Mendes EW, Silveira RC. Massage therapy improves
         neurodevelopment outcome at two years corrected age for very low
         birth weight infants. Early Hum Dev 2009.

(142)   Burns E, Zobbi V, Panzeri D, Oskrochi R, Regalia A. Aromatherapy in childbirth: a pilot randomised controlled trial. BJOG 2007; 114(7):838-844.

(143)   Freedman FB. Yoga Biomedical Bulletin: Quarterly Journal of Yoga Biomedical Trust [35]. 1997.
         Ref Type: Journal (Full)

(144)   Dr Jill Bolte Taylor. http://www.ted.com/index.php/talks/jill_bolte_taylor_s_powerful_stroke_of_insight.html. 2011. TED conferences. Accessed 2008
         Ref Type: Internet Communication

(145)   Taylor JB. My Stroke of Insight: A Brain Scientist's Personal Journey. New York, NY: Penguin Books; 2009.

(146)   Beddoe AE, Paul Yang CP, Kennedy HP, Weiss SJ, Lee KA. The effects of mindfulness-based yoga during pregnancy on maternal psychological and physical distress. Journal of Obstetric, Gynecologic, and Neonatal Nursing 2009; 38(3):310-319.

(147)   Beck U. Risk Society: Towards a New Modernity. Sage Publications Ltd; 1992.

(148)   Ensler E, Steinem G. The Vagina Monologues. London: Virago; 2001.

(149)   Ensler E. Insecure at Last: Losing It in Our Security-Obsessed World. New York, NY: Villard Books; 2006.

(150)   Parratt J, Fahy K. Trusting enough to be out of control: a pilot study of women's sense of self during childbirth. Australian Journal of Midwifery 2003; 16(1):15-22.

(151)   Diego MA, Jones NA, Field T, Hernandez-Reif M, Schanberg S, Kuhn C et al. Maternal psychological distress, prenatal cortisol, and fetal weight. Psychosom Med 2006; 68(5):747-753.

(152)   Entringer S, Kumsta R, Hellhammer DH, Wadhwa PD, Wust S. Prenatal
         exposure to maternal psychosocial stress and HPA axis regulation in
         young adults. Horm Behav 2009; 55(2):292-298.

(153)   Field T, Diego M, Hernandez-Reif M, Vera Y, Gil K, Schanberg S et al.
         Prenatal maternal biochemistry predicts neonatal biochemistry. Int J
         Neurosci 2004; 114(8):933-945.

(154)   Field T, Diego M, Hernandez-Reif M, Gil K, Vera Y. Prenatal maternal
         cortisol, fetal activity and growth. Int J Neurosci 2005; 115(3):423-429.

(155)   O'Connor TG, Heron J, Glover V. Antenatal anxiety predicts
         child behavioral/emotional problems independently of postnatal
         depression. J Am Acad Child Adolesc Psychiatry 2002; 41(12):1470-
         1477.

(156)   O'Connor TG, Ben-Shlomo Y, Heron J, Golding J, Adams D, Glover
         V. Prenatal anxiety predicts individual differences in cortisol in pre-
         adolescent children. Biol Psychiatry 2005; 58(3):211-217.

(157)   Van den Bergh BR, Marcoen A. High antenatal maternal anxiety is
         related to ADHD symptoms, externalizing problems, and anxiety in 8-
         and 9-year-olds. Child Dev 2004; 75(4):1085-1097.

(158)   Weinstock M. The potential influence of maternal stress hormones
         on development and mental health of the offspring. Brain Behav
         Immun 2005; 19(4):296-308.

(159)   Coussons-Read ME, Okun ML, Nettles CD. Psychosocial stress
         increases inflammatory markers and alters cytokine production across
         pregnancy. Brain Behav Immun 2007; 21(3):343-350.

(160)   Hardy R, Wadsworth ME, Langenberg C, Kuh D. Birthweight,
         childhood growth, and blood pressure at 43 years in a British birth
         cohort. Int J Epidemiol 2004; 33(1):121-129.

(161)   Odent M, Odent P. http://www.wombecology.com. Accessed 2010.
        Ref Type: Internet Communication

(162)   Jacobson B, Eklund G, Hamberger L, Linnarsson D, Sedvall
        G, Valverius M. Perinatal origin of adult self-destructive behavior. Acta
        Psychiatrica Scandinavica 1987; 76(4):364-371.

(163)   Raine A, Brennan P, Mednick SA. Birth complications combined with
        early maternal rejection at age 1 year predispose to violent crime at
        age 18 years. Arch Gen Psychiatry 1994; 51(12):984-988.

(164)   Salk L, Lipsitt LP, Sturner WQ, Reilly BM, Levat RH. Relationship of
        maternal and perinatal conditions to eventual adolescent suicide.
        Lancet 1985; 1(8429):624-627.

(165)   Al-Mufti R, McCarthy A, Fisk NM. Survey of obstetricians' personal
        preference and discretionary practice. European Journal of
        Obstetrics, Gynecology, and Reproductive biology 1997; 73(1):1-4.

(166)   Kendrick KM, Da Costa AP, Broad KD, Ohkura S, Guevara R, Levy
        F et al. Neural control of maternal behaviour and olfactory recognition
        of offspring. Brain Res Bull 1997; 44(4):383-395.

(167)   Levy F, Kendrick KM, Goode JA, Guevara-Guzman R, Keverne EB.
        Oxytocin and vasopressin release in the olfactory bulb of parturient
        ewes: changes with maternal experience and effects on
        acetylcholine, gamma-aminobutyric acid, glutamate and
        noradrenaline release. Brain Res 1995; 669(2):197-206.

(168)   van LE, Kerker E, Swanson HH. Inhibition of post-partum maternal
        behaviour in the rat by injecting an oxytocin antagonist into the
        cerebral ventricles. J Endocrinol 1987; 112(2):275-282.

(169)   Carmichael MS, Humbert R, Dixen J, Palmisano G, Greenleaf W,
        Davidson JM. Plasma oxytocin increases in the human sexual
        response. J Clin Endocrinol Metab 1987; 64(1):27-31.

(170)   Young LJ, Wang Z, Insel TR. Neuroendocrine bases of monogamy. Trends Neurosci 1998; 21(2):71-75.

(171)   Kosfeld M, Heinrichs M, Zak PJ, Fischbacher U, Fehr E. Oxytocin increases trust in humans. Nature 2005; 435(7042):673-676.

(172)   Fischer-Shofty M, Shamay-Tsoory SG, Harari H, Levkovitz Y. The effect of intranasal administration of oxytocin on fear recognition. Neuropsychologia 2010; 48(1):179-184.

(173)   Marsh AA, Yu HH, Pine DS, Blair RJ. Oxytocin improves specific recognition of positive facial expressions. Psychopharmacology (Berl) 2010; 209(3):225-232.

174)   Rimmele U, Hediger K, Heinrichs M, Klaver P. Oxytocin makes a face in memory familiar. J Neurosci 2009; 29(1):38-42.

(175)   Bartz JA, Hollander E. Oxytocin and experimental therapeutics in autism spectrum disorders. Prog Brain Res 2008; 170:451-462.

(176)   Jacob S, Brune CW, Carter CS, Leventhal BL, Lord C, Cook EH, Jr. Association of the oxytocin receptor gene (OXTR) in Caucasian children and adolescents with autism. Neurosci Lett 2007; 417(1):6-9.

(177)   Opar A. Search for potential autism treatments turns to "trust hormone". Nat Med 2008; 14(4):353.

(178)   Nissen E, Lilja G, Widstrom AM, Uvnas-Moberg K. Elevation of oxytocin levels early post partum in women. Acta Obstet Gynecol Scand 1995; 74(7):530-533.

(179)   Gaskin IM. Home Birth—Why It's Necessary . 14-1-2007. Ina May Gaskin Productions.
         Ref Type: Internet Communication

(180)   Odent.M. The Long Term Consequences Of How We Are Born. Primal Health Research 14[1]. 2006.

(181)   Beckmann MM, Garrett AJ. Antenatal perineal massage for
        reducing perineal trauma. Cochrane Database of Systematic Reviews
        2006;(2):CD005123.

(182)   Sun YC, Hung YC, Chang Y, Kuo SC. Effects of a prenatal yoga
        programme on the discomforts of pregnancy and maternal childbirth
        self-efficacy in Taiwan. Midwifery 2009.

(183)   Beddoe AE, Lee KA. Mind-body interventions during pregnancy. J
        Obstet Gynecol Neonatal Nurs 2008; 37(2):165-175.

(184)   Cyna AM, Andrew MI, McAuliffe GL. Antenatal self-hypnosis for labour
        and childbirth: a pilot study. Anaesth Intensive Care 2006; 34(4):464-
        469.

(185)   Fields N. Yoga: empowering women to give birth. Pract Midwife 2008;
        11(5):30-32.

(186)   Bergstrom M, Kieler H, Waldenstrom U. Effects of natural childbirth
        preparation versus standard antenatal education on epidural
        rates, experience of childbirth and parental stress in mothers and
        fathers: a randomised controlled multicentre trial. BJOG 2009;
        116(9):1167-1176.

(187)   Ernst E. Funding research into complementary medicine: the situation
        in Britain. Complement Ther Med 1999; 7(4):250-253.

(188)   Zollman C, Vickers A. What is complementary medicine? BMJ 1999;
        319(7211):693-696.

(189)   Pascali-Bonaro D. Orgasmic Birth. 6-1-2009.
        Ref Type: Motion Picture

(190)   Dick-Read G. Childbirth without Fear: the principles and practice of
        natural childbirth. 4th ed ed. London: Pinter & Martin; 2004.

(191)   Kuh D, Ben-Shlomo Y. A Life Course Approach to Chronic Disease
        Epidemiology. 2nd ed ed. Oxford: Oxford University Press; 2004.

(192) O'Brien PMS, Wheeler T, Barker DJP, Royal College of Obstetricians and Gynaecologists (Great Britain), Royal College of Obstetricians and Gynaecologists (Great Britain), Study Group. Fetal programming influences on development and disease in later life. London: RCOG Press; 1999.

(193) deMause L. The Emotional Life of Nations. New York: Other Press LLC; 2002.

(194) Uvnäs-Moberg K. Oxytocin, the Inner Guide to Motherhood. The Mid-Atlantic Conference on Birth and Primal Health Research; 2010.

(195) Uvnäs-Moberg K. The oxytocin factor: tapping the hormone of calm, love, and healing. Cambridge, Mass: Da Capo Press; 2003.

(196) Pedersen CA. Biological aspects of social bonding and the roots of human violence. Ann N Y Acad Sci 2004; 1036:106-127.

(197) Horta BL, Bahl R, Martinés JC, Victora CG. Evidence on the long-term effects of breastfeeding. World Health Organization; 2007.

(198) Layard PRG, Dunn J, Good C, I. A good childhood searching for values in a competitive age. London: Penguin; 2009.

(199) Davies E. French feminists row over rise of 'ideal mothers'. The Guardian 2010 Feb 13; Sect. International:21.

(200) National Childbirth Trust. http://www.nct.org.uk. 2009.
Ref Type: Internet Communication

Lightning Source UK Ltd.
Milton Keynes UK
UKOW051125060213

205910UK00001B/249/P